Better
Sailing

Other Books by Richard Henderson

- First Sail For Skipper
- Hand, Reef and Steer
- Dangerous Voyages of
     Captain William Andrews (Ed.)
- Sail and Power (with B. S. Dunbar)
- The Racing-Cruiser
- Sea Sense
- The Cruiser's Compendium
- Singlehanded Sailing

Better Sailing

Error Analysis in Sailing and Seamanship

Richard Henderson

Contemporary Books, Inc.
Chicago

This book is dedicated to
Harold R. White

Published simultaneously in Canada by
Beaverbooks
953 Dillingham Road
Pickering, Ontario L1W 1Z7
Canada

Illustration on title page from *The Mariner's Catalog*
published by International Marine Publishing Company

Contents

Introduction

The primary purpose of this book is to point out, analyze, and suggest corrective measures for the most common errors in sailing and yacht seamanship. In addition, the book will explain some recent changes and developments in sailing techniques that sometimes run counter to standard advice and may lead to confusion and misunderstandings. The errors to be discussed run the gamut from serious and possibly dangerous blunders to subtle mistakes that affect speed and sailing efficiency. Certain lapses in seamanship might even seem amusing, but usually only to the spectator, seldom to the perpetrator.

In regard to the author's qualifications, the reader can rest assured that he is receiving advice from someone who is highly experienced, because in more than forty-five years of sailing I have made almost every conceivable mistake. What few errors I have not committed myself, I have seen others make. During approximately thirty years of my sailing career I have kept logs or at least brief notes about my experiences afloat, and these jottings point out the numerous times I have gone astray.

One can always learn firsthand by trial and error, of course, but it is much less painful to learn about common failings and pitfalls by reading of the mistakes made by others. Hence this book.

1

Potential Problems and Errors

Not so long ago, I wrote to an old friend—one of the best and most experienced seamen I know—about my plan to do a book on error analysis in sailing. He wrote back, "If you run out of mistakes, just say the word, and I'll send you a couple of thousand." Of course, my friend's remark was made with tongue in cheek, but only partially so. For, old salt that he is, he realizes that no one who sails a boat is above making mistakes. What is the reason for this high potential for errors? Primarily, it is that sailing depends on the vagaries of wind, water, and boat behavior; thus errors can never be entirely eliminated. They certainly can be minimized, however, through analysis and study, proper application of knowledge gained from experience, and the development of good habits.

Lacks and Lapses in the Basics

Novice sailors most often make mistakes because of deficiencies in training, lack of education, and inexperience; but veterans most often commit errors because of complacency, overconfidence, and especially forgetfulness of lessons learned and basic seamanship. Thus it is important that sound basics be learned by beginners and periodically reviewed by veterans. Modern junior sailors are fortunate that they can avail themselves of many excellent junior training programs sponsored by leading yacht clubs. Adult tyros do not have this advantage, but they can enroll in one of the many sailing schools or, of course, take one of the boating courses offered by the U.S. Coast Guard Auxiliary and the U.S. Power Squadrons. In addition to taking practical instruction, the beginner—or the experienced sailor—can gain a great deal of valuable information from magazine articles and books. Every serious sailor (or any kind of boatman, for that matter) should have a reference library. Two reliable sources for building a library are the Dolphin Book Club, Camp Hill, Pennsylvania 17012 and International Marine Publishing Company, 21 Elm Street, Camden, Maine 04843.

It is not the purpose of this book to cover elementary seamanship. The basics appear in some of my earlier books, such as *Hand, Reef and Steer*. However, the rest of this section is devoted to some of the most common violations of fundamentals that often lead to trouble.

Improper Garb

Many young sailors go barefoot, but they sometimes suffer stubbed toes, splinters from docks, or skids on a wet deck as a result. Proper skidproof boat shoes are a must. A hat that affords ample shade is also important to avoid sunburn and possible sun poisoning or skin problems (which can result when certain people with fair skin are exposed to the sun over a long period of time). Be sure the hat is fitted with a lanyard, because many have been blown overboard. When cruising, have at least one pair of long trousers and a long-sleeve shirt to protect against overexposure to the sun. It is helpful if the breast pocket of the shirt can be buttoned shut, as this pocket is famous for losing sunglasses and other articles. Don't wear jackets that are overly bulky or that have a lot of straps or belts that can get caught on things. An important part of the seaman's garb is a pocket knife with a folding marlinespike. This useful tool is inexpensive, easy to carry, and could be vital in an emergency; yet surprisingly few sailors carry one.

Faulty Small Boatmanship

Coast Guard statistics continue to show that a great many accidents occur in small open boats. Quite often dinghies swamp or capsize from overloading. If your boat is moored offshore and you use a dinghy to go aboard, don't try to save an extra trip by overloading, and be sure that the dinghy is properly trimmed. It is not unusual to see such boats loaded down by the stern to such an extent that a sizable powerboat wake could swamp them. Heavy outboard motors on small dinghies increase this problem, especially when the operator moves aft; and if the engine stalls, the bow will swing downwind and present the dangerously low stern to the waves. Incidentally, Coast Guard regulations now require a personal flotation device for every person on almost any kind of boat, but from my experience it is unusual to see yachtsmen in dinghies with PFDs (buoyant cushions will do). If you should happen to swamp or capsize, remember the oft-repeated advice to stay with the boat. Don't try to swim for a "nearby" shore.

A less serious but nonetheless frequent and highly annoying mistake in handling a rowing boat is coming alongside without unshipping the oarlocks. Many topsides have been marred because of this lapse in elementary seamanship. In this day of outboard motors, handling a pair of oars is rapidly becoming a lost art.

Improper Knots

Common lapses are forgetting how to tie important knots or using them improperly. The bowline is undoubtedly the most essential knot; yet some sailors have to relearn it at the beginning of each boating season. The main problem seems to be in forming the initial loop, but if you start by tying a simple overhand knot and then pull the short end of the line, the loop will naturally form the right way (see Figure 1-1).

The square knot is another important knot, but some sailors inadvertently make granny knots when they are not looking at what they are doing or when tying the knot in the dark. I have done this myself. Then too, a square knot is sometimes incorrectly used to join two lines that will be under consider-

FIGURE 1-1: A QUICK, SURE WAY TO TIE A BOWLINE

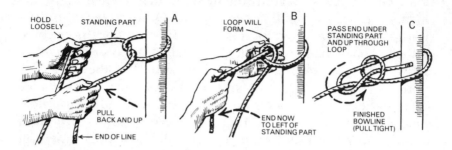

able strain. A far better knot is the sheet bend, which is closely related to the bowline.

The clove hitch is frequently used to make a boat fast to a piling, but if a real strain comes on the line, the knot is positively dangerous, for it can slip. Should you use a clove hitch for this purpose, always put an extra hitch or two around the standing part of the line.

The warning that a sheet should never be hitched on its cleat is well known. It originated in the days when lines were made of vegetable fibers that could swell and cause a jam when wet. Even when using modern synthetic line, I think it is usually better not to hitch a sheet. Halyards, though, are a different matter. I have seen halyards come off their cleats; so if the line is dacron, which does not swell, I definitely think hitches should be used. Be sure, however, to put ample figure-eight wraps around the cleat before the line is hitched; otherwise the hitch could jam.

Failure to Check the Weather

Quite often inexperienced sailors get into trouble because they neglect checking the weather reports before setting off for a day's sail or a weekend cruise. With up-to-date weather maps on television and the availability of radio weather, such as the continuous reports over VHF (162.55, 162.40, and 163.274 MHz), there is seldom an excuse for not being generally well informed. Every cruising boat should carry a weather radio (preferably one that is crystal-tuned to the VHF stations) and a barometer. Many modern sailors do not make proper use of the barometer, but the instrument can tell a great deal. As the old master Cornelius Shields has written, "I think that a yachtsman who fails to consult his barometer at least twice a day doesn't deserve to win races." I might add that the instrument is also important for those who do not race. In addition, it is important to watch the sky constantly, especially in westerly directions in middle latitudes. Look for signs of an approaching front or the building of cumulus clouds that could develop into thunderheads, particulary on hot, humid summer days. A good seaman can usually be identified by his ever-roving weather eye. If tide or current is a major factor in your area, of course, it should also be checked carefully before and while sailing.

Mistakes in Sailing Fundamentals

Errors relating to the fine points of sail trim and shaping, sail handling, and steering will be discussed in later chapters, but here I'll mention a few of the most common mistakes having to do with the basics of sailing.

Beginners often have maneuvering problems because they fail to keep sufficient way on their boats. Slowing down as a matter of caution or for some other reason will definitely weaken the flow of water against the rudder. The sailor must remember that a certain amount of speed is necessary for steering control.

A common misconception regarding basic sail trim is that sails should be kept at right angles to the wind when sailing downwind. A much better practice is to keep an angle of attack (the angle the apparent wind makes with an extension of the boom, as shown in Figure 1-2) at approximately 30 degrees so that the sail will continue to produce effective lift for as long as possible when bearing away to a running course. This means that the luff will be kept on edge (on the verge of luffing), and telltale yarns attached to the luff of the sail will be streaming aft without excessive flutter or twirling. Luff yarns and trim angles will be discussed in Chapter 3.

Another sailing error when going downwind is to luff up in

FIGURE 1–2: UTILIZING LIFT
WHEN BEARING AWAY FROM A
BEAM REACH

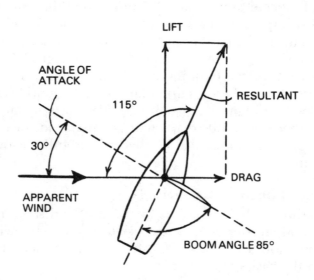

strong gusts rather than bearing off. If it is necessary to stop excessive heeling in a strong puff, the mainsheet should be slacked, of course, but it is often a mistake to luff up suddenly when sailing below a beam reach, because centrifugal force will increase the heeling. Bearing away promptly, however, before the boat has reached a high angle of heel, will increase stability, partly because the centrifugal force will tend to counteract heeling (see Figure 1-3). Also, it should be obvious that a boat is most stable when her end rather than her side is exposed to the wind, and she can seldom be held bow to the wind for more than a few moments. Thus the stern should face the wind unless it is necessary to lower or reduce the mainsail.

Incidentally, it is not always realized that heeling can be reduced on a boat having an unballasted centerboard by partially raising the board. This raises the center of lateral resistance (CLR), thereby reducing the heeling arm, the vertical distance between the CLR and the center of effort (the geometric center of the sails). For a given wind pressure, the heeling moment is reduced when the arm is shortened (see Figure 1-4). In heavy weather, centerboards should almost never be raised all the way, however, because the boat will generally make too much leeway or lose directional stability and also because the board acts as a roll damper.

Jibing in a breeze is a maneuver that is excessively feared by many beginners and even many veterans. Some boats are difficult to tack in heavy weather with very rough seas, and sails can be damaged from violent flogging when one attempts to turn the boat through the eye of the wind. If this is the case, a properly executed jibe may very well be the preferable ma-

**FIGURE 1–3: UPWIND
VERSUS DOWNWIND TURN**

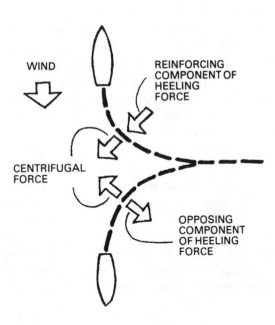

WIND

REINFORCING
COMPONENT OF
HEELING
FORCE

CENTRIFUGAL
FORCE

OPPOSING
COMPONENT
OF HEELING
FORCE

FIGURE 1-4: EFFECT OF DRAFT ON HEELING ARM

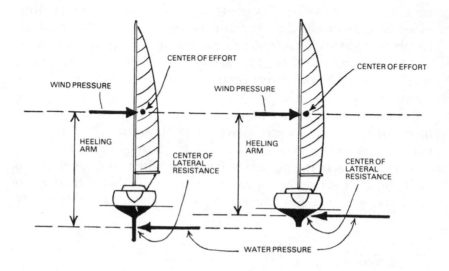

neuver. Jibing a keelboat normally requires shortening the mainsheet and having the boom bowsed down when it crosses the centerline of the boat. On a small centerboarder, however, it is usually better to leave the sheet cleated and grab the entire mainsheet tackle (rather than hauling in just one part of the tackle) so that the boom can be thrown over and the sheet payed out in the fastest possible time. This technique requires great care to see that the mainsheet does not foul; and there should be an on-center boom vang (attached at the base of the mast) set up tight to prevent the boom from riding up and causing a so-called Chinese jibe (in which the lower half of the sail jibes while the upper half does not). Be sure the main boom is not so long that it will strike the backstay if it should happen to ride up. When the wind is so strong that there is considerable risk of damaging the rig or capsizing in a centerboarder, the mainsail should be lowered before jibing. For subsequent upwind efficiency, the main, deeply reefed, may be hoisted again after wearing around on the opposite tack.

Lack of Lead, Log, and Lookout

My nautical dictionary calls the three Ls of navigation (*lead, log,* and *lookout*) a "motto of eternal vigilance." Lack of vigilance in the three Ls can, of course, lead to groundings and/or collisions. It may not be necessary actually to sound with a lead line or use a distance recording log, but certainly every skipper should know, in a general way, the depth of his waters and where he is at all times. Many a sailor, including myself, has run aground because of failure to consult his charts, lack of attentiveness to landmarks and navigation aids, or overconfidence in familiar waters. Failure to keep a continual lookout on crowded waters is downright dangerous for reasons that should be obvious. However, it is quite easy, especially on a sailboat, to relax one's vigilance when distracted or when lulled into a false feeling of security by the fact that sailboats move relatively slowly and the fact that they usually have the right of way over powerboats. Then, too, the helmsman's vision is often blocked by sails. It is a serious but not uncommon error to relax the lookout when the boat is privileged, especially when she is sailing on the starboard tack and has the right of way over another sailboat on the port tack. When converging with another boat, it is always safest to assume that you are not seen. Incidentally, I have only occasionally seen a horn carried within easy reach of the helm on a sailboat, but a horn should be handy, especially when the boat is under power. It may be needed to call attention to yourself and to comply with the Rules of the Road. Low-cut deck-sweeping jibs should not be carried unless there is a permanent lookout on duty to warn the helmsman of approaching vessels behind the jib.

Rules of the Road

It is surprising how many boatmen do not really know the Rules of the Road. Junior training programs very often concentrate on racing rules at the expense of the Rules of the Road. Many junior sailors (and adults as well) think that a starboard-tack sailboat always has the right of way over a

A modern fiberglass version of the classic Folkboat. Note the large window in her genoa to alleviate the problem of poor visibility on the lee bow.

port-tack boat, but in actuality, under the present U. S. Inland Rules, the closehauled boat has the right of way over one running free regardless of which tack the boats are on. Some sailors are also under the impression that sailboats always have the right of way over motor craft. Of course, this is not true when the sailboat overtakes a boat under power, and she is not allowed to hamper a large vessel under power in a narrow channel.

A not uncommon but potentially dangerous mistake is for a privileged boat to make changes in course and/or speed when approaching a burdened vessel. This is wrong, because the burdened boat cannot take proper avoiding action unless the other vessel moves in a predictable way. Just about the only time when a boat with right of way should change her course or speed is "in extremis," when collision seems imminent. Another factor a sailboat skipper should consider is that powerboat skippers may not fully understand the maneuvering principles involved in sailing. A sudden tack or jibe near an approaching motorboat could lead to confusion and a possible collision.

Foolish Fueling

Although this book is about sailing, many sailboats have auxiliary power, and some dangerous fueling practices should be
mentioned. In general, many sailors are too casual about filling their gasoline tanks. They may get away with careless
practices for a long time, but they are risking serious injury
and/or boat damage from explosion or fire. In observing boats
taking on fuel at gas docks, I have noticed that portholes and
the companionway hatch are seldom closed to prevent fumes
from flowing below, and boats very often pull away from the
dock before their bilges and engine rooms are thoroughly
sniffed and adequately aired.

Every gasoline powered boat with an inboard engine should
have a bilge blower. It should be installed high above the
bilge, because gas fumes will sink and a spark could ignite
them, and it should be run before starting the engine (whether
or not the boat has just taken on fuel) until no odor of fumes
is emitted through the exhaust vent. Very often the blower is
not run for long enough, and its vent is not sniffed for fumes.
Be sure the suction hose, which should extend to the low
point of the bilge, does not have its end covered with bilgewater and that the hose is not bent in such a way that water
will become trapped inside and block the flow of air (see Figure 1-5).

FIGURE 1–5: SOME COMMON REASONS FOR TRAPPED
GASOLINE FUMES

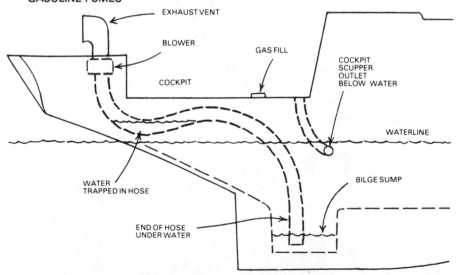

EXHAUST VENT

BLOWER

GAS FILL

COCKPIT
SCUPPER
OUTLET
BELOW WATER

COCKPIT

WATERLINE

WATER
TRAPPED IN HOSE

BILGE SUMP

END OF HOSE
UNDER WATER

Many boats have their fill pipes in the bottom of the cockpit (a construction feature I deplore), and should your boat have such an arrangement, be sure the cockpit scupper outlets are not under water. If they are, fumes cannot escape through them. If the scupper outlets cannot be raised above the water by removing crew or moving their weight forward, thoroughly fan the fumes out of the cockpit. Also be sure that the gas tank and all fuel pipes are grounded. There should be a flexible hose between the fill pipe and the tank to prevent possible cracking of the pipe from fatigue due to vibration, but see that there is a jumper wire between a nonconductive hose and the tank. More information on safe fueling (as well as other safety-related subjects) can be obtained from my book *Sea Sense,* and further details appear in the rather formidable book *Safety Standards for Small Craft* published by the American Boat and Yacht Council.

Mistakes in Fitting Out

Troubles are often experienced, especially by beginners and new boat owners, as a result of what might be called misfitting out. Very often insufficient or improper gear is carried, and sometimes it will be incorrectly installed or put in the wrong location. In some cases a boat may even have too many fittings, which can clutter the deck or lead to unnecessary complexities. Mistakes in fitting out may be the fault of the designer, the boat builder, the sales agent, the service yard, or the owner, who may make the wrong selection or choose inadequate gear. Very often a new boat owner will overeconomize, thinking that initially he can get by with less than the minimum of equipment he will really need. The following shortcomings are the ones I have most often noticed on new boats and even on many old and supposedly well-found and well-tuned boats.

Rigging and Related Fittings

A common general error having to do with the rig is the mismatching of fittings and lack of uniformity in strength. It is not unusual, for instance, to see a boat equipped with heavy shrouds and small turnbuckles or perhaps a heavy shackle holding a tiny block. The standing rigging on a modern boat should be envisioned as a chain that is only as strong as its weakest link. Of course, the links consist of the wire rigging, the shackles, blocks, turnbuckles, toggles, and so forth, which fail under a load of 8,000 pounds, for example, it makes no sense to have a shroud that will support 16,000 pounds. Actually, if any part of the rig were to be oversize, it would be best to have extra large turnbuckles. These fittings are probably less predictable than others due to the fact that they are threaded, and sometimes they are bent when the boat is brought alongside a dock.

The various parts of the standing rigging are connected by pins, and these are sometimes the wrong size—too long, too short, or too small in diameter for the holes they pass through. Using a pin that is too small in diameter results in point loading, or a greater than necessary stress at one point (see Figure 1-6, A). A pin that is too short may shear off its cotter (see Figure 1-6, B), while a pin that is too long may get pressed against an adjacent object and also shear its cotter. Sometimes a shroud tang will be bent slightly upward to accommodate a long pin as shown in Figure 1-6, C, and when the shroud becomes loaded, the pin will be forced out of its hole. Another occasional fault is the placement of a hole for a pin too close to the edge of the tang, which will be under strain (Figure 1-6, A).

Be sure to avoid the flexing of terminal rigging fittings and consequent risk of fatigue failure of wire or fittings by using ample toggles, which act as universal joints (see Figure 1-6, D). Toggles are usually needed at the lower ends of all shrouds (between the chainplates and turnbuckles), at the lower ends of stays, and at the upper end of the jib stay. This stay is subject to considerable lateral deflection from the jib and from the spinnaker pole when it strikes the stay or bears against it on a close reach. Most boats are now being fitted with lower toggles but seldom with uppers. Incidentally, toggles should be kept lubricated so that they can move easily. Frequently overlooked areas are the lifeline terminals, which should have toggles when they are fitted with turnbuckles. However, I prefer that the ends of lifelines be lashed with stout lines, as this avoids the need for toggles, turnbuckles, and pelican hooks, which can open accidentally. And incidentally, breaking the metallic continuity of the lifelines may very well improve the accuracy of your radio direction finder. Lashings can be cut quickly with a sharp knife in an emergency, such as when it is necessary to haul aboard a person who has fallen over the side.

Split pins (as shown in Figure 1-6, F) are nearly always the safest cotters to hold rigging pins in place or prevent turnbuckles from untwisting. Cotter rings, also illustrated, are sometimes handy, but I have seen them work loose, and in one case I know about, they were responsible for a dismasting. In addition, these rings can work their way out of spring-loaded shackle pins, causing the fitting to fall apart; so if rings are used, they should be taped as shown in Figure 1-6, F. Locknuts, sometimes used on turnbuckles, are a double risk, because vibration can cause them to work loose and back off, and if they are set up very tight, they put added stress on the turnbuckle threads. Split pins will stay put after they are inserted and bent, but they are perhaps the greatest cause of torn sails (to say nothing of scratched crew members) and so great care must be taken to keep them taped or otherwise covered. A common error is to use permanent cotters of a material that is incompatible with the pins they penetrate. This practice is particularly dangerous with ground tackle that is submerged in salt water because of the probability of galvanic corrosion. For a turnbuckle that needs constant adjustment, I find it handy to use shower curtain rings for easily removable cotters, but they need careful watching and periodic renewal.

Quite often turnbuckles are installed in a nonuniform way so that one turnbuckle is screwed to the right to tighten the rigging while another must be screwed to the left to tighten. Normally, installations should be such that right-hand or clockwise turning causes the rigging to tighten. Turnbuckles

FIGURE 1–6: SOME RIGGING DETAILS

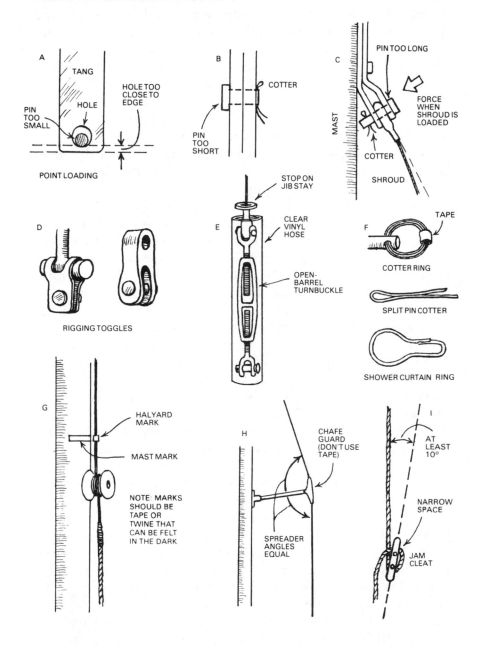

A

TANG

HOLE

HOLE TOO CLOSE TO EDGE

PIN TOO SMALL

POINT LOADING

B

COTTER

PIN TOO SHORT

C

MAST

PIN TOO LONG

FORCE WHEN SHROUD IS LOADED

COTTER

SHROUD

D

RIGGING TOGGLES

E

STOP ON JIB STAY

CLEAR VINYL HOSE

OPEN-BARREL TURNBUCKLE

F

TAPE

COTTER RING

SPLIT PIN COTTER

SHOWER CURTAIN RING

G

HALYARD MARK

MAST MARK

NOTE: MARKS SHOULD BE TAPE OR TWINE THAT CAN BE FELT IN THE DARK

H

CHAFE GUARD (DON'T USE TAPE)

SPREADER ANGLES EQUAL

I

AT LEAST 10°

NARROW SPACE

JAM CLEAT

that are upside down, so to speak, should be inverted to assure uniformity. Beware of turnbuckles with solid barrels, because these make it difficult to judge how far the threaded rods are screwed in, and also they require lock nuts, which are undesirable for the reasons already mentioned. Open barrels (such as the type shown in Figure 1-6, E) are much safer. Boots are often used to cover turnbuckles to protect against corrosion and cover cotter pins, but I prefer clear plastic tubes rather than opaque boots. A tube can be cut from large-diameter, clear vinyl hose, which allows constant visibility of the turnbuckle and easy accessibility to the fitting for servicing by sliding the tube upward (see Figure 1-6, E).

Many boats are not adequately fitted with stops at the ends of tracks and at halyard terminal eyes to prevent them from being pulled into their sheaves. Important tracks that need stops are the mainsheet traveler, sail slide and gooseneck tracks, jib sheet leads, jiffy reef cheek blocks, and the spinnaker pole track. Without these stops the slides can run off their tracks. Halyard stops can sometimes be made from large split washers that will prevent wire halyard eyes from being pulled into their sheaves. If a stop cannot be fitted, then the halyard should be marked with tape or twine near the deck to indicate when the sail is fully hoisted. The usual manner is to mark the mast and to align the halyard mark with the one on the mast (see Figure 1-6, G).

Another place where a stopper is often needed is just above the top of a jib stay turnbuckle when the lower hanks of the sail will jam on the terminal swaged fitting of the stay. A split washer or possibly a neoprene shackle guard may be used (see Figure 1-6, E).

Keepers in the form of fairlead eyes are often needed aloft to prevent external halyards from fouling or jumping out of their sheaves. Fairleads are also needed on other parts of the running rigging wherever there is potential for harmful chafe.

Another part of the rigging that requires attention is the spreaders. These are frequently neglected, although their failure can cause a dismasting. Wood spreaders are subject to rot, and their top surfaces, never seen from the deck, are very often not adequately protected with varnish or paint. It may be a good idea to cover the top surfaces with aluminum paint so that most of the heat and sunlight will be reflected away. Periodically examine the spreaders, especially the inboard and outboard ends, for rot and splits. See that the outboard ends are well seized to the shrouds and that the spreader exactly bisects the shroud angle (see Figure 1-6, H). There should be adequate chafe guards at the spreader tips to protect the genoa jib, but don't wrap the tips with boat tape, because it will harden with exposure to the sun and chafe the sail. Use soft felt, rubber boots, or spreader rollers. Be cautious about aluminum spreader sockets, because a number of them have failed. It is generally safer to have sockets of stainless steel, but when the spars are aluminum, there should be a barrier material such as plastic tape between the two different metals to prevent possible galvanic corrosion.

Beginners and even some experienced sailors occasionally get into trouble because of a runaway halyard. Sometimes the wire portion of a wire and rope halyard is sufficiently heavy to

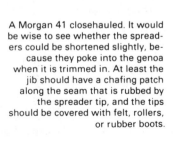

A Morgan 41 closehauled. It would be wise to see whether the spreaders could be shortened slightly, because they poke into the genoa when it is trimmed in. At least the jib should have a chafing patch along the seam that is rubbed by the spreader tip, and the tips should be covered with felt, rollers, or rubber boots.

make the end of the halyard run aloft unless it is secured. An unsecured halyard can also be lost if someone yanks down on the luff of a sail when it is being lowered and the halyard coil fouls and fails to uncoil. The whole tangle is then pulled aloft. Beginners often lay a coil on the deck the wrong way so that the line feeds off the bottom rather than off the top of the coil, and of course, this is asking for trouble. Secured halyard ends are a safeguard against such accidents. The usual way of securing is to run the end of the halyard through a hole or space in the base of the cleat and tie a stopper knot. A good way of doing this is explained in Chapter 2 and Figure 2-6. Another bitter end (extreme end) that needs attaching is that of the anchor rode. Neglect of this important principle nearly cost me my anchor and rode during a storm many years ago. If the rode is chain, it is wise to lash the bitter end rather than shackle it, because a lashing can often be cut more quickly in an emergency.

More often than not, boats are fitted with the wrong kind or size of cleats placed in the wrong locations. A symmetrical arrangement of cleats on each side of the cockpit is seldom possible, because with the usual clockwise-turning winches, sheets will lead off the outboard side of the winch on the starboard side and the inboard side of the winch on the port side. A jam cleat similar to the conventional cleat but having a narrow space under one horn is a handy type, but occasionally it is installed the wrong way. The narrow space should be facing the winch so that the line can be wrapped first around the horn with the wider space, then jammed under the opposite horn (see Figure 1-6, I). Many times cleats are not properly angled to the direction from which the line pulls, and this fault can cause unwanted jamming. The axis of the cleat should be angled at least 10 degrees away from the direction of the line as shown in Figure 1-6, I. Also there should be a space of at least a foot and a half between the cleat and its winch whenever possible. Cleats are often placed where they can foul lines. Some vulnerable areas are on the fore side of the mast and on the cabin top. Mast cleats should be located as far as possible to the sides of the mast so that the jib will not foul them during a tack. Cabin top cleats can sometimes be clam or cam-action types that are less subject to being fouled. It is a good idea to label (normally with a labeling gun) all cleats for running rigging.

Aside from cleats, several other kinds of fittings and gear can foul lines and thus cause trouble. Some usual offenders are anchors stowed on the foredeck, spinnaker poles stowed on side decks, forward ventilators, and winch handle holders located where the handles can be snagged by lines. A satisfactory location for the anchor is often on the cabin top abaft the mast, or sometimes a Danforth anchor can be stowed forward of the headstay with the stock across the top of the bow pulpit. Many cruising boats are now fitted, with a roller chock at the stem to support a plow anchor, and this is a very practical arrangement. A tall bow ventilator should be easily removable so that it cannot be fouled by the jib when tacking. Spinnaker pole chocks and similar fittings should be well rounded so that they cannot snag lines. Winch handles. which are especially susceptible to being fouled, are often best stowed in winch base compartments. Handles for the mast winches can sometimes be stowed effectively inside Dorade vents that are located just abaft the mast on either side of the cabin top. A frequent problem when tacking is the fouling of jib sheet shackles on shrouds. "J" hooks (made by Barient) are not likely to foul, but they are expensive, and any kind of jib sheet shackle can strike a crew member in the head when the sail is flogging. For this reason, I prefer that the sheets be tied with bowlines, but they must be tied so that they face the right way to avoid fouling (see Chapter 2 and Figure 2-1, C).

New stock boats with standard equipment are usually fitted with winches that are at least one size too small. If economy dictates the choice between two large and four small sheet winches in the cockpit, I would far rather have two large, preferably two-speed winches with ratcheting handles. Reel halyard winches, which wind up and self-stow their halyards on reels, can be dangerous for reasons that will be explained in Chapter 2. If this type of winch is used, I strongly recommend the screw-toggle brake control that allows gradual easing of the halyard and permits hoisting with the brake on. Care should be taken to see that sheets lead to their winches at the proper angle, otherwise overrides and consequent jamming of the sheets on the winch drums are likely. A sheet should not be led down to a winch. Normally it should be led very slightly up to the winch or at right angles to the turning axis of the drum. It is hard to believe, but some new boats have their winches placed so close to lifeline stanchions that the winch handles cannot be turned 360 degrees. This should never be tolerated. Either the winches or the stanchions should be moved. In some cases slightly shorter winch handles might be used, but they will provide somewhat less power. Another occasional fault is the location of mast winches where they will block the full turn of the roller reefing handle.

Since the advent of synthetic lines that do not swell when wet, boats have more and more often been fitted with undersized blocks for modern running rigging. Use of blocks that are too small is a bad practice for two reasons. First, there may not be a sufficient margin of safety in the strength of the blocks and second, if wire rope is used, a small-diameter sheave can weaken the wire. Be sure all blocks are hefty and that each one has a metal strap running between the eye from which it is hung and the sheave pin (sometimes this is not the case). There is nothing that will break a block more quickly than putting a side load on it when it is not free to swivel. Don't try to economize by using a nonswiveling block when you need one that swivels. In some cases, however, adding extra shackles may solve the problem.

Turning blocks are usually necessary to relieve side loading and extra upward strain on a rail-mounted genoa lead block. The usual turning block is located fairly far abaft its winch, and this means the sheet will lead from the rail track lead block to the after turning block and thence forward to the winch so that the sheet will make a turn of nearly 180 degrees. This will double the load on the turning block. For example, a 500-pound load on the clew will put a 1,000-pound strain on the block. It is evident, therefore, that turning blocks should be tremendously strong; yet this is not always the case on some of the cheaper stock boats. The best kind of turning block is the so-called foot block, and it should be solidly through-bolted with a sizable backing plate.

As a matter of fact, all fittings should be bolted whenever possible. A few years ago a young sailor in my area died from a blow to the head inflicted by a fitting that pulled loose. Be sure to check the security of your fittings, and never station yourself or a crew member where injury could result from the failure of a fitting. A certain amount of caution should be exercised, too, in using side-opening snatch blocks. Compared with equivalent solid blocks, snatch blocks may not be as strong, and excessive violent shaking may cause them to open. I would especially advise against using snatch blocks for the leads of a storm jib when tacking in heavy weather.

I think it is very important that the layout of running rigging be based on the assumption that the boat will sometimes be sailed short-handed. This is a realistic consideration for most boats, especially if they are daysailers or cruising boats. Such an assumption requires that all sheets be within reach from the helm, that the boat have a topping lift running from the boom end to the masthead, and that all spinnaker lines (halyard, sheet, guys, and lift) be controllable from the cockpit. It may also be a good idea to have the main halyard led aft, but I am opposed to leading the jib halyard aft, because it is easier for one person to hand this sail when its halyard is secured at the mast. More will be said about handing sails in Chapter 2.

Cockpit Installations

Some important installations in or near the cockpit that are frequently inadequate or unsatisfactory are the bilge pump, scuppers, engine controls, ventilators, and compass.

Bilge Pump. Too often one sees a small-capacity bilge pump mounted inside a cockpit seat locker. This is a poor location, because the locker lid must be opened to operate the pump, and obviously this destroys the watertight integrity of a self-draining cockpit. One happy solution to this problem is to

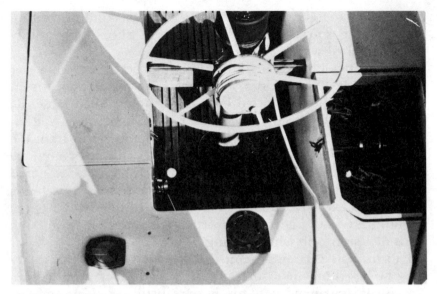

Cockpit details on the author's Ohlson 38. The dark square to the right of the wheel is an open seat locker containing the main battery switch. This arrangement allows the engine to be started from the helm. The throttle and gear shift seen inside the cockpit well at the left-hand corner could be better recessed, as they are vulnerable to being kicked. The dark object on deck directly abaft the wheel is an access plate to the head of rudder post, to which an emergency tiller can be fitted. The dark object on deck near the left-hand corner of the cockpit is a bilge pump; a handle is easily inserted to allow the helmsman to pump while he is steering. The drum on the wheel is for self-steering. (Photograph, R. C. Henderson.)

FIGURE 1–7: COCKPIT BILGE PUMP

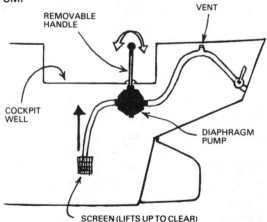

use a diaphragm-type pump such as the Whale or Henderson (not related to the author), which has a capacity of 10 gallons per minute or better. These pumps can be installed satisfactorily in the deck or in the cockpit sole, perferably near the helm. The pump handle is removable, and a proper installation is leakproof. I would strongly recommend a coarse screen or strum box at the bottom of the intake hose to keep the pump from being clogged with sediment, and the outlet should be high above the waterline (often through the transom if it is a conventional type) with a high vented loop in the discharge line to prevent back-siphoning (see Figure 1-7). Any outlet that will be submerged will need a shut-off valve. For offshore sailing I would have another permanent bilge pump operable from the cabin.

Scuppers. Drains and scuppers are seldom adequate, and often they are put in the wrong locations. Some common faults are (1) scuppers in the cockpit sole too small and placed aft where they can admit water to the cockpit when the boat is moving fast enough to draw a large quarter wave (see Figure 1-8); (2) deck scuppers not at the low points when the boat is normally trimmed so that there is often a puddle of water trapped by the rail; and (3) inadequate drainage of cockpit seats, winch base lockers, and gutters under seat locker lids. Scuppering must be ample at the corner where the seat joins the cockpit coaming; otherwise a puddle can form when the boat heels (see Figure 1-8). All scupper pipes that penetrate the hull below or close to the waterline should be fitted with seacocks, and hoses should be attached to the cocks with double screw-type hose clamps wherever possible. Even large cockpit scuppers take a surprisingly long time to drain a cockpit that has filled from a boarding sea; thus a companionway with a low sill needs a substantial lower storm slide to keep water out of the cabin. Incidentally, the forward end of the sliding hatch over the companionway is a usual source of leaks, so be sure there is a watertight scabbard into which the hatch cover can slide (see Figure 1-8).

FIGURE 1-8: WATERTIGHTNESS AND DRAINAGE

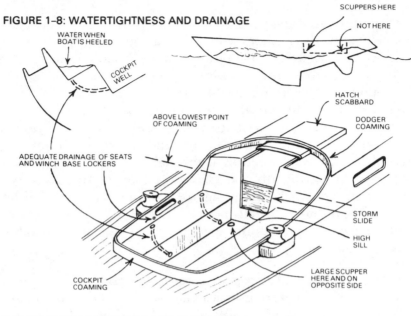

WATER WHEN
BOAT IS HEELED

COCKPIT WELL

SCUPPERS HERE

NOT HERE

ADEQUATE DRAINAGE OF SEATS
AND WINCH BASE LOCKERS

ABOVE LOWEST POINT
OF COAMING

HATCH
SCABBARD

DODGER
COAMING

STORM
SLIDE

HIGH
SILL

COCKPIT
COAMING

LARGE SCUPPER
HERE AND ON
OPPOSITE SIDE

A boat with its cockpit awash. Some boats sink surprisingly low by the stern when their cockpits are filled. To lessen the danger of sinking, a boat with a self-bailing cockpit and a low companionway sill needs a lower storm slide such as the one shown here. (Photograph, William W. Cross.)

Engine Controls. The main objections I have to most installations of engine controls are (1) there seldom are enough instruments; (2) some controls are not located near the helm; and (3) controls are often too exposed so that they can be bumped, stepped on, or snagged with a line. Important gauges that are often missing are a tachometer (this is especially important if the boat has no speedometer), an ammeter, and an oil pressure gauge. Two important controls that are sometimes not accessible from the helm are the battery main switch and the fuel shut-off valve. In my opinion this lack of accessibility is a mistake, because if the boat is being sailed short-handed, the helmsman should be able to start the engine at a moment's notice without leaving his station. He should also be able to shut down the engine completely by himself without leaving the helm. Incidentally, some boats have two batteries charged with an alternator, and a three-way switch permits running the engine on one or the other or both. When operating such a boat, don't pass through the "off" position to change from one battery to the other with the engine running, because this could burn out the alternator diodes. Also, be sure the engine is off or idling before switching from battery 1 to battery 2. The battery switch and fuel valve might be located just inside the companionway if the helmsman's position is at the forward end of the cockpit, but these controls might be in a handy seat locker if the helm is aft. For heavy-weather offshore sailing, I prefer that the starter button be inside the companionway, because a sea filling the cockpit can and has shorted out the starting motor. On our boat we have dual starter buttons, one in the cockpit and one below, with the former being disconnected for offshore work.

Cockpit engine controls should be protected by being recessed into the side of the cockpit well. The throttle is especially vulnerable to being moved inadvertently by someone's kicking it or by its being fouled with a line. Thus I prefer the control that has a removable handle and a notched hub that can be turned without the handle such as the kind made by Morse.

Ventilators. Gasoline engines need venting in accordance with Coast Guard regulations, but it is astonishing to see the way this is done on some sailboats. Quite often the intake vent faces forward and is located on the side deck. It is usually permanently secured so that it cannot be turned to face aft, and there is no provision to block off the vent. Of course, this means that when the boat heels and submerges her rail or gets heavy spray on her deck, water will run aft and directly into the vent. One salesman at a boat show told me that this was perfectly acceptable because the water would merely run into the bilge. Evidently he didn't recognize the disadvantages of a continually filling bilge. If a boat has vents that are vulnerable to flooding, there should certainly be a means of blocking them off in heavy weather. Even vents that lead to a gasoline engine should be closed temporarily when they are admitting solid water and when the engine is not running. If a vent cannot be easily removed and its hole closed with a screw plate, it might be closed with a fitted wood plug.

Compass. A good compass is the seaman's most valuable instrument, yet many installations are poor, especially on small boats. Too often compasses are not aligned accurately so that their fore-and-aft lubber lines (the reference marks or posts on a compass bowl that indicate the heading) are exactly on or parallel to the centerline of the boat. Also, a helmsman may very well need more than the usual forward and aft lubber lines on a sailboat compass; 45-degree or at least 90-degree lubber lines are almost essential, because the helmsman seldom sits directly behind the compass when the boat is heeled, especially when spray is coming over the windward rail.

Whenever possible, I think a binnacle should be installed. A binnacle raises the compass to provide better visibility and a greater distance from ferrous objects and electrical gear that cause deviation. Furthermore, a raised compass usually makes it easier to take bearings without the need of another instrument (a pelorus or hand-bearing compass), and the navigator can use a center-pivot extension or shadow pin for sun azimuths (useful for celestial navigation and compass adjusting).

Care must be taken, however, to see that the binnacle is not placed where it can be fouled by the mainsheet. Sometimes a curved bar guard may be placed above the compass to protect it and also to provide a handrail for steadying oneself in heavy weather. In some cases, if a binnacle is impractical, dual flush-mounted compasses may be installed in the after end of the cabin house, one on each side of the companionway.

To minimize errors from deviation, compasses should be located at least three feet from any electronic equipment and six feet from sizable iron objects such as the engine. Electric wiring that must be near the compass should be twisted with each conductor wound around the other to help cancel out their magnetic fields. Be sure you get a compass that can remain horizontal on its gimbals at high angles of heel. I have actually seen powerboat compasses installed on sailboats. When you check your compass for deviation, do it under sail and under power. Errors may be caused by the running engine and also by the angle of heel.

Other Cockpit Equipment. Other important cockpit items are a ring or horseshoe buoy mounted near the helmsman and a tiller extension and/or helmsman's seat. The buoy must be mounted in such a way that it can be quickly lifted from its holder in case someone falls overboard. Occasionally, the buoy is snapped on, jammed in, or even lashed to its holder, and this might mean that it could not be thrown in time to be reached by the person overboard. The tiller extension and helmsman's seat are often needed on a boat with a high cabin trunk to improve visibility. Of course, the extension also allows the helmsman to sit further to windward where he can place his weight more effectively while getting a better view of the luff of the jib. For the same reasons, steering wheels should be of sufficient diameter to allow the helmsman to sit reasonably far to windward, and he should also be able to move outboard to leeward in order to glance periodically to leeward of the jib for lookout purposes. Finally, be sure any slippery areas that will be stepped on are skidproofed by applying anti-slip tape or by some other means.

So far, only the mistakes in fitting out above deck have been discussed, and these are the ones that most often seem to cause trouble for the daysailing skipper. But errors, omissions, and inadequacies also can occur below deck, and these will be discussed in Chapter 6, which deals for the most part with cruising seamanship.

Procedures

Once a new boat owner or beginning sailor learns the correct operational procedures (from books, instructor, boat manuals, and so on), he should write them down in a log or ship's notebook. Procedural errors in such matters as getting underway and securing the boat most often occur because of forgetfulness and oversights. The best means of overcoming these mistakes is with checklists in the notebook. This book should also contain a stowage plan (telling where all gear is kept), information about equipment (the lengths of docking lines and anchor rodes, the size of various sails, tank capacities, and so on), and operating instructions for certain equipment (stove, head, engine). A notebook of this kind is invaluable not only to the owner, but to his crew, guests, charterers, or anyone else who uses the boat.

Of course, checklists and operational procedures will vary with individual boats, but the following lists might be considered representative samples for a medium-sized cruising sailboat.

Getting Underway

   • Unlock all hatches [note combination for lock or location of key]. Stow lock [designate location].
   • Open seacocks (except for any sink or head that will overflow when the boat is heeled). [Give locations of seacocks and operating instructions—for example, "pull handle up" or "turn wheel counterclockwise".]
   • Open hatches and ports if weather permits.
   • Pump bilge [designate location of pump].

• Remove binnacle and winch covers. Stow covers [designate location].

• Strike (lower) dodger for maximum visibility.

• Remove sail cover(s), fold, and stow [designate location].

• Remove halyard gilguys (lines tying halyards away from mast). Stow gilguys [designate location].

• Bend jib and its sheets [designate stowage location] and temporarily stop the jib. [Designate location of stops.]

• Install lead blocks [designate stowage location], and see that track slide is in correct position. [Lead positions for all headsails should be clearly marked and labeled.]

• Lead sheets through blocks and knot ends.

• Remove anything from the foredeck that could foul the jib or its sheets.

• Untie mainsheet coil, see that the topping lift is properly set, and attach main halyard shackle to headboard.

• Break out winch handles and outhaul crank [designate stowage location] and stow in winch base lockers or holders.

• Adjust mainsail outhaul and see that battens are securely in their pockets before hoisting.

• See that all loose gear is securely stowed (so that it will not fall when boat heels) and that locker doors are closed and latched.

• Check level of engine lube oil [designate location of dipstick].

• Check fuel supply, either from notations in logbook or by measuring with dipstick through fill pipe. [Designate location of fill pipe and dipstick and explain marks on dipstick.]

• Turn on fuel valve [designate location] before starting engine.

• Turn on battery main switch [designate location].

• Turn on bilge blower if gasoline engine [designate location] and run for about five minutes.

• Put hand over blower exhaust outlet [designate location] to be sure air is coming through, and sniff the outlet for gas fumes.

• Insert gear shift lever and throttle handle [designate stowage location].

• Start engine [give basic instructions] and let it run for a few minutes before casting off.

• Check engine exhaust to see that cooling water is flowing through.

Securing

• Be sure that mooring pendant is properly secured. Cleat pickup line over pendant eye to hold it on cleat. [Check docking lines if boat is kept in a slip. See that there is the proper amount of slack in lines. Check knots, chafe guards, and fenders.]

• If engine is running, put gear in neutral and let idle for a few minutes before shutting down. [It is a common mistake to cut off the engine at once, allowing a sudden buildup of residual heat.]

• Shut down engine: turn off ignition, close fuel valve, turn off main switch, and close water intake valve [indicate locations].

• Stow gear shift and throttle handles [designate where].

• Slack mainsail outhaul. Stow crank handle [designate where].

• Furl, stop, and cover mainsail. (Cover goes *under* halyards.)

• Coil and hang mainsheet.

• Secure tiller.

• Unbend jib. Bag with tack up and pendant attached. Stow [designate where].

• Stow winch handles and snatch blocks [designate where].

• Stow boathook, deck swab, and cushions [designate where].

• Strike all flags [unless you want to leave one at masthead to keep off birds]. Stow [designate where].

• Put on binnacle and winch covers.

• Tie off halyards with gilguys.

- Coil and hang the ends of all halyards.
- Dog hatches and ports (but allow air into cabin through ventilators and louvered or otherwise vented companionway slide).
- See that ventilators are turned the correct way [designate which].
- Pump bilge and head.
- See that pressure is off the stove and check L. P. gas cylinder valves, if there is a gas stove [designate where].
- Open icebox and lockers that need ventilation [designate which].
- Remove trash and any food that can spoil.
- Shut off seacocks, except for scuppers, and all electrical switches.
- Enter engine hours and any information about repair or equipment needs in the logbook.
- Insert companionway slides and lock.
- Raise dodger (if necessary to allow ventilation but keep out water).
- Lock cockpit seat lockers.
- Stow all keys [designate where].

2

Sail Handling

At best, errors in sail handling are a handicap for the racer and a cause of inconvenience for the cruiser, but at worst they are a source of damage and even danger. It is easy enough to have occasional problems when one has learned the correct procedures for handling sails, but without this knowledge any sailor, especially the neophyte in heavy weather, is really asking for trouble.

Bending and Hoisting Sails

Incorrect bending of a sail will usually not cause any serious problems, but some mistakes can cause real damage. Occasionally, a hank or sail slide will be put on upside down, and when the sail is hoisted and the halyard winched tight, the luff can be ripped. To avoid this problem, run the luff through your hand to see that it is not twisted when you are bending on, and be sure that all hanks are facing the same way when they are clipped to the stay. Another more common mistake is to tack the jib down to a location too far abaft the stem or to use a long tack pendant that does not hold the tack close to the jib stay. Either practice puts excessive strain on

**FIGURE 2–1:
BENDING
SAIL**

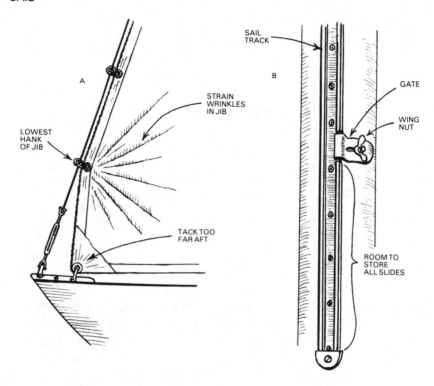

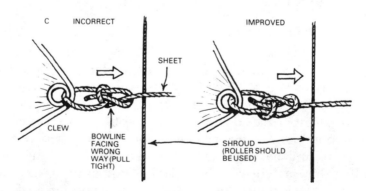

From *Singlehanded Sailing,*
published by International Marine
Publishing Company

the lowest hank, sometimes breaking it or tearing the luff (see Figure 2-1, A).

Of course, a jib should be bent on from tack to head, because clipping on the hanks from head to tack would require the extra effort of holding the top hanks up while the lowers are being attached. Thus a jib should always be bagged head or clew first with the tack at the top of the bag so that it can be found immediately and shackled to the stemhead. It is not always easy to hank on a jib at the bow when a boat is pitching in a seaway. The best practice is to kneel or squat, getting your center of gravity low; then straddle the sail with one leg and pull the sail forward through your legs as the hanks are being clipped onto the stay. The straddle stance will help prevent the jib from blowing overboard.

Many sailors do not realize that a mainsail can be bent on in the same manner as the jib—working from tack to head—if a gate is installed near the bottom of the mast track (Figure 2-1, B). The operation is a lot easier when it is done this way, because obviously the top slides will not have to be held up as they would if the bending were done from head to foot. The gate must be high enough so that the section of track below it can accommodate all the sail slides. Another big advantage of having a gate is that a storm trysail or another heavy-weather sail can be bent on while the mainsail is up, saving time and effort when a sail change must be made.

Jib sheets nowadays are usually attached with bowlines—a good idea because these knots will seldom shake loose, and they eliminate the need for a hard shackle that can cause serious injury to a crew member when the sail is flogging in a breeze. Be sure, however, that the bowlines are turned the proper way so that they will not snag on the shrouds. If the loop of the knot that goes around the standing part of the sheet faces the shroud, it may snag, but when the loop is facing away from the shroud there is seldom if ever a problem with fouling (see Figure 2-1, C). Of course, large shroud rollers will discourage fouling in any event, but rollers of large diameter cause unnecessary windage and disturb the airflow through the jib slot.

A fundamental rule for hoisting is always to look aloft before hauling on the halyard, and to look up periodically while the head of the sail is going aloft. If you watch the sail go up, you can usually prevent a halyard from getting hooked around the spreaders, correct a twisted hank before any damage is done, or prevent a batten from becoming caught under a shroud. A problem I often had in a recent long ocean passage was having the halyard blow off to leeward and become snagged on the spreader tip. Such fouling is not uncommon on a boat with short spreaders when she is rolling in a seaway. I found it was necessary to keep tension on the hoisting part of the halyard by pulling down on it and then pulling down on the luff of the sail until the head was about three or four feet up the mast. The purpose of the tension is obviously to keep slack out of the halyard so that it cannot be blown or whipped off to leeward.

Of course, it is advisable to keep a boat headed directly into the wind when her mainsail is being hoisted, but this is not always possible, and sometimes the wind will be coming from broad on the bow. In this case, the sheet should be slacked so that at least the sail itself is headed directly into the wind. With many new stock cruising boats that have long booms, however, the main boom cannot be swung broad off when the mainsail is not fully hoisted, because there is no proper topping lift. Common practice is to hang the main boom from a short wire strap clamped to the permanent backstay. I would certainly recommend that the new boat owner having such an arrangement do away with it and install a proper topping lift running from the end of the boom to the masthead. The lift can be adjusted from the end of the boom or from the mast if the lift can be run from the boom end along (or possibly through) the boom to the mast or is led from a block aloft down the mast. The latter arrangement, using a dacron rope lift, is preferable on a cruising boat, because the lift can be used as a spare halyard. The rope will not be weakened by running it over a small sheave as would be the case with a wire lift. A racer might not want the additional windage of an extra line running down the outside of the mast, and so an along-the-boom arrangment, which allows lift adjustments when the boom is broad off, might be most satisfactory, unless the boat is equipped with roller reefing. In this case, the lift must be attached to a swivel at the boom end to avoid wrapping the lift around the boom when it is being turned to roll in a reef.

The problem of a topping lift chafing the mainsail leech seldom occurs if elastic shock cord is used to keep slack out of the lift. A method of rigging the shock cord that is usually adequate is illustrated in Figure 2-2, A. If the mainsail has an exceptionally large roach or if the clew goes out to the very end of the boom, the lift can be unclipped from the boom end and clipped to a ring seized or clamped with a compression sleeve to the backstay. However, great care must be taken to remember to refasten the lift to the boom before lowering sail. Furthermore, when there is any possibility that the mainsail will have to be lowered in a hurry, the lift should not be removed from the boom end. A long length of shock cord may also be rigged from the topping lift to the backstay in the manner illustrated (Figure 2-2, B), but it may tend to hold the boom in on a light-air run.

FIGURE 2–2: MASTHEAD TOPPING LIFTS

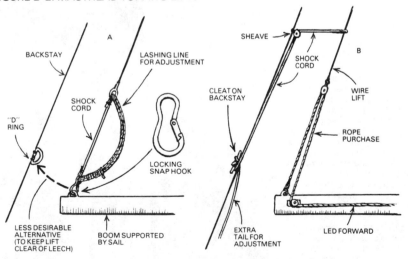

Trouble-free hoisting of sails requires complete familiarity with halyard winches, especially the reel type that stores the wire on its drum. This kind can be extremely dangerous if it is not handled carefully. Occasionally a serious accident occurs when the operator or another crew member is hit on the head with the winch handle. This can happen if the handle slips out of the operator's hand while the halyard is under tension or if the brake is released while the handle is still in the winch. For maximum safety be sure that (1) the handle is a lock-in type, (2) it is always gripped firmly, (3) it is never left in the winch when not in use, and (4) the brake is never released with the handle in (unless someone is holding the handle tightly). Most important of all, be sure that no one gets his head, arms, or legs within the turning radius of the handle in the event that the brake should slip or accidentally be released.

A modern reel halyard winch with screw-toggle brake release at the bottom of the winch base (on the left-hand side). This design allows gradual easing of the brake and the hoisting of the mainsail with the brake on. Notice the step-up rim just above the winch base; it is intended to take the last few turns of the wire after the sail is almost fully hoisted in order to prevent the final turn from jamming into the loosely packed turns on the main drum. (Photograph, R. C. Henderson.)

I prefer the screw-toggle type of reel winch, which allows a gradual easing of the brake and permits hoisting with the brake on. When sail is hoisted with the brake tightened, the handle will not whirl around even if it slips out of the operator's hand, and the screw toggle allows a gradual easing of the brake when sail is being lowered. Be sure that the wire halyard is guided from one end of the drum to the other when hoisting so that the wire will be evenly distributed over the drum and not pile up on one side. Also, the last few turns of the wire should be guided into the step-up rim, so that halyard tension will not force the wire into the loose underlying turns and possibly cause a jam.

Conventional (non-reel) winches used with wire halyards having rope tails require the use of head pendants on short-luff sails in order that the wire part of the halyard will adequately reach the winch. There really should be four or five turns of wire around the winch; otherwise the tail splice joining the wire and rope can pull apart when the halyard is under great tension. This is not likely when the splice is well made, but I have actually seen it happen. Quite often a crew member will wrap a tail splice around the winch, but this practice can be harmful to the splice. Be sure there is ample space between the winch and the halyard cleat, so that the splice can be positioned between the two and will not have to be bent around either the winch or the cleat.

Incidentally, when a crew member is ordered to crank in on a winch, he should do so as quickly as possible, and this means that he should not uncleat the line until after the cranking has been done. Too often crew members uncleat and then crank, but this wastes valuable time.

Shortening Down and Changing Sails
One of the most troublesome aspects of sail handling is matching the sail area to the strength of wind. This must be done, however; otherwise the boat will be overpowered in a strong wind and underpowered in light air. Of course, the usual means of altering sail area is by reefing or by changing headsails. With multimasted rigs, total area is often reduced

by simply lowering one sail, but many expert seamen believe that this often is not the best solution. Probably one of the most common mistakes in sailboat seamanship is to hand the mainsail in heavy weather while a large headsail is left flying. I have done this myself in the past and have been lucky enough to get away with it, but the fact is that such a practice lessens the strength of the mast and subjects it to possible breakage. It is far better to drop the headsail and leave the main up or, preferably, reef the main slightly and change to a smaller headsail. The reason is that a sail attached at many points along a mast distributes the pressures more evenly and holds the mast steady, helping prevent whipping in a seaway. On a yawl or ketch it might be all right to drop the main temporarily during a sudden squall when there is a working jib set, but prolonged sailing in a blow with the main down and a large headsail set is really asking for trouble. Another reason for not sailing a yawl or ketch under jib and mizzen alone is that the rig is very inefficient, especially when beating to windward. The wide space between sails results in harmful backwind and upwash (bending of the streamlines) and an ineffectual slot.

The most common method of reefing today is the so-called jiffy reef, which is really a simplified version of the old points system. The latter makes use of reef points—short lines that hang down from eyelets that are set in a row from luff to leech at the location on the mainsail where the reef is desired. A frequent error in using reef points is to tie them around the boom, a practice that can cause the sail to tear or be strained as a result of varying tension on the points. The correct method is to tie the points under the foot of the mainsail (an area that can absorb the nonuniform tension) or else to use one continuous lacing line rove through the eyelets and around the boom. Jiffy reefing forgoes the reef points, and quite often the bunt of the sail (the portion taken in during reefing) is simply left to hang down below the boom. However, this is not really a seamanlike practice when the reef is deep, and it is preferable that at least a few eyelets and a lacing line be used to hold the bunt up against the boom and perhaps help take some of the belly out of the middle of the reefed sail. If the bunt is left hanging down, try to keep it hanging on the windward side of the boom; otherwise the fold of cloth could fill with water from heavy rain or spray.

There are many methods of rigging the leech and luff cringles in jiffy reefing. I prefer the leech arrangement illustrated in Figure 2-3, which uses a section of track and a sliding cheek block fastened to the side of the boom. This fitting is made by Nicro/Fico and Merriman Hollbrook, Inc. Notice that the reefing line (more correctly termed the *earing*) can be tied to the cheek block post; and then the line is run under the boom to the opposite side, up through the reef cringle, and down to the cheek block sheave and thence forward. Of course, there might be another track with a sliding eye on the side of the boom opposite the sliding cheek block, but the arrangement illustrated in Figure 2-3 is the simpler. Some advantages of having sliding cheek blocks are that (1) they are easy to position correctly through trial and error, (2) mainsails can be changed without adding new permanent cheek blocks, and (3) if the boat is fitted with roller reefing, the jiffy alternative can be used without abandoning the infinite variability of the roller system. When it is desirable to roll in a reef, the cheek block can be slid aft where it will not be wrapped by the sail. On our boat we can use either roller reefing, jiffy reefing, or both alternately. Of course, this dual reefing arrangement prohibits having a winch on the boom to tighten the leech earing, but a mast winch can be used if the earing is led forward to a block at the gooseneck, down to another block at the base of the mast, and thence up to the mast winch. If one wants to roll the boom after jiffy reefing, a short line around the after end of the boom is substituted for the jiffy earing. This sounds complicated, but it is quite easily done.

Newcomers to jiffy reefing, if they don't use sliding cheek blocks, frequently install fixed blocks (and eyes on the opposite side of the boom) in the wrong location—usually too far forward. Eventually these fittings have to be moved, and sometimes they are moved several times before the correct location

FIGURE 2–3:
JIFFY REEF
SLIDING
CHEEK BLOCK

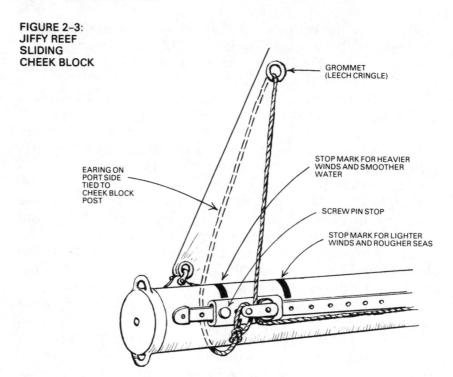

GROMMET
(LEECH CRINGLE)

STOP MARK FOR HEAVIER
WINDS AND SMOOTHER
WATER

SCREW PIN STOP

STOP MARK FOR LIGHTER
WINDS AND ROUGHER SEAS

EARING ON
PORT SIDE
TIED TO
CHEEK BLOCK
POST

FIGURE 2–4:
POSITIONING A FIXED
CHEEK BLOCK

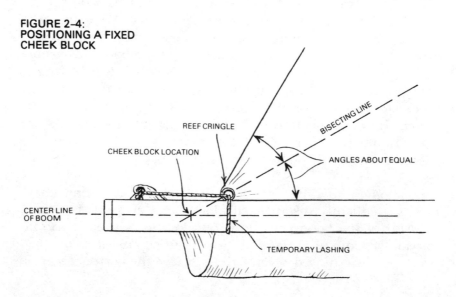

REEF CRINGLE

BISECTING LINE

ANGLES ABOUT EQUAL

CHEEK BLOCK LOCATION

CENTER LINE
OF BOOM

TEMPORARY LASHING

is found. A simple rule of thumb method for finding the right location is illustrated in Figure 2-4. First, the sail is hoisted with the luff and leech jiffy reef cringles lashed down to the boom. An outhaul line is run to the after end of the boom, and the reefed foot is pulled taut. Then the angle between the leech and the reefed foot is bisected, and the point where an extension of the bisecting line intersects the centerline of the boom will give a good indication of where the cheek block (and eye on the opposite side) should be located. What you want to do is apply almost equal tension on the leech and foot. Actually, you may want a little more tension on the foot to help flatten the sail and ease the upper leech in a strong blow when the seas are not too rough, and this would require that the cheek block be slightly further aft. In slightly less winds with rough seas, however, the block usually should be about on the bisecting line for moderate draft and a bit of extra power. Of course, having the cheek block on a track will allow some flexibility of adjustment for varying conditions. One must be careful, however, that the slide can be securely locked in the selected position.

There might be considered two methods of jiffy reefing, one for small boats (perhaps those under twenty-five or thirty feet long) and another for larger craft. On the former, the boom end is raised up to the leech cringle by hauling on the clew earing after the mainsheet has been completely slacked, and then the halyard is slacked until the luff cringle can be secured to the tack with a hook or tack earing. On large boats, however, the luff is usually reefed first and then the leech. Of course, this method requires a topping lift to hold the boom up when the halyard is slacked. Sometimes the skipper of a medium-sized boat will use the small-boat method of hauling the clew up to the cringle before slacking the halyard, and this is a mistake, because it can stretch or strain the leech. Another disadvantage of the small-boat method is that completely slacking the sheet will cause maximum flogging, which does a sail no good in a blow. In such conditions, by the way, batten pockets should have been lashed or taped closed, for I have had battens in offset pockets thrown out of the sail when it was flapping violently.

A Cal 28 surfing in a blow. The reefed main has a deep crease just forward of the battens, a common problem with deep roller reefing. The set of the sail might have been improved by pulling aft on the leech when the boom was being turned. In heavy weather especially, one must be careful of lines overboard that might foul the propeller should the engine be needed. (Photograph, Joe Fuller.)

Roller reefing can work very well when the reef is not too deep, and, as said before, the method has the advantage of being infinitely variable; that is to say, sail can be reduced any slight amount to balance the helm properly. Deep reefs, however, cause problems, because the middle of the sail bags out or gets creases due to the inability to apply outhauling tension, and the end of the boom inevitably begins to droop down, unless the boom has a larger diameter at its after end. Furthermore, a deeply rolled in reef can stretch out the leech, unless a topping lift is kept taut to relieve the strain.

Rather than rolling in a very deep reef, it is often advisable, for cruisers at least, to set a large storm trysail or a smaller mainsail—perhaps a Swedish main having a hollow leech (reverse roach) and a slightly shorter foot but a long luff. The gate in the track (previously discussed) is particularly handy for changing to the trysail or small main, because either of these sails can be bent on beneath the normal mainsail. Then, when a change is required, the mainsail is dropped, its slides are run off the track, and the smaller sail bent on beneath can be hoisted just as soon as the halyard is transferred. We used this method on a recent ocean passage, and it worked very well. If you don't have a heavy-weather main or trysail, it is preferable to roll in a moderate reef rather than a deep one and set a headsail one size smaller than the size appropriate for a deeply reefed main.

In choosing a smaller jib for moderately heavy weather, it is important to bear in mind that strong winds are usually accompanied by heavy seas, and the headsail should afford plenty of drive. Since most of the thrust comes from the forward part of the sail, it is highly beneficial to use a jib with a long luff. Until fairly recently, it was customary to set a short-luff genoa in heavy weather, but several years ago sailmaker Charles Ulmer began to publicize the merits of the long-luff, short-footed jib, and now most other sailmakers seem to concur. Although the tall, narrow sail keeps the center of effort fairly high, most of the heeling force comes from the area just ahead of the leech; and if that area can be kept fairly far forward by reducing the overlap, side force that causes heeling is minimized. Furthermore, the sail with a short foot keeps the center of effort forward to help counteract the weather helm induced by heeling, and the sail is easier to handle when tacking. Instead of the conventional number 3 genoa, it is usually much better to have a nearly full-luff lapper (a slightly overlapping jib) with a moderately high clew (to keep the foot clear of the bow wave).

A fairly recent fad is reefing genoa jibs. This is a relatively easy way of shortening down, but I am opposed to the practice, because it can stretch the sail out of shape. I have seen a good genoa damaged from reefing. The method might be used satisfactorily for short periods of time on a heavy-weather genoa that is strongly reinforced, but the heavy cringle and reinforcing patch on the leech will not help the set of the sail. Furthermore, a reefed jib will not have the best shape and camber for heavy weather. The so-called Venetian jib reefing system uses a special jib cut with a very high clew so that only the luff needs to be reefed. This method is much less harmful to the sail, but its unreefed (as well as reefed) shape is less than optimal, and sheet leads need drastic changing.

The usual manner of changing a headsail is to hank on the replacement jib under the one that is hoisted. Normally, all the hanks of the replacement sail will fit under the lowest hank of the hoisted jib, but if not, of course, the bottom hank will have to be unsnapped. A sheet and lead block are supplied for the new jib, and then the hoisted sail is lowered, its hanks being unsnapped as it comes down. When the head is within reach, the halyard is transferred to the replacement jib, the lowered sail is cleared from the top of the one to be hoisted, and the new jib can then be raised. It is helpful if there is some kind of net between the deck and lifelines forward to keep the sails lying on the foredeck from washing overboard.

Many cruising sailors make this operation a great deal more difficult than necessary by keeping the boat headed close to the wind when headsails are being changed. It is much easier to lower and hoist a replacement jib if the boat is momentarily run off before the wind, because the apparent wind is less, the motion is easier, and the forward sails are partially blanketed. Of course, a racer making sail changes while beating to windward cannot use this method, but a cruiser need not be too concerned about losing such a slight amount of ground to windward.

Many of the most modern racing boats use a double-slotted headfoil system for changing jibs. Such foils fit over existing forestays or replace them. They have full-length slots that accept luff boltropes, which take the place of traditional hanks. The major advantages of this system are an aerodynamically cleaner rig and the ability to change headsails without lowering the raised jib before the new one is hoisted. As the various slotted foils have been improved, problems have become less frequent, but occasional difficulties still occur—jamming, frictional resistance, the boltrope escaping from its groove, some plastic foils melting slightly from friction, or the sail sliding overboard because it has no hanks to hold its luff during the lowering operation. Also, special care must be taken not to let the spinnaker pole slam against the foil, as some kinds have been dented or cracked as a result. Perhaps the foils that cause fewest difficulties are aluminum ones that have side-by-side grooves rather than fore-and-aft grooves. Fore-and-aft grooves require that the foil be turned when sails are changed (see Figure 2-5). On the other hand, I have heard consistently good reports about the Stearn roller furling foil, which has fore-and-aft slots (Figure 2-5). In systems using plastic foils, there has been some trouble with the boltropes slipping out of or occasionally melting the foils, and grooved stainless steel rods are more subject to cracking from fatigue. With the exception of breakage on a twelve-meter boat, however, I have heard of very few problems with aluminum extrusions.

It seems that the most common difficulties with slotted foil sail changes are jamming and frictional resistance. Hoisting and lowering may require great effort because of sails sticking together, especially when they are wet, and luffs or boltropes sometimes bind in the slots or in the feeding mechanisms near the tack. Friction and jams can be alleviated by (1) keeping the bolts tight on the feeder box and having a crew member

FIGURE 2–5: HEADFOILS AND ATTACHMENTS   From *Singlehanded Sailing*, published by International Marine Publishing Company

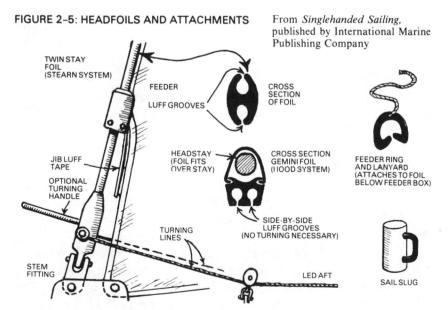

TWIN STAY FOIL (STEARN SYSTEM)

FEEDER

LUFF GROOVES

CROSS SECTION OF FOIL

JIB LUFF TAPE

OPTIONAL TURNING HANDLE

HEADSTAY (FOIL FITS OVER STAY)

CROSS SECTION GEMINI FOIL (HOOD SYSTEM)

FEEDER RING AND LANYARD (ATTACHES TO FOIL BELOW FEEDER BOX)

TURNING LINES

SIDE-BY-SIDE LUFF GROOVES (NO TURNING NECESSARY)

STEM FITTING

LED AFT

SAIL SLUG

help the sail into the feeder ring and feeder, (2) having the feeder box sufficiently high off the deck, (3) using Teflon tape on the sails' luffs, (4) getting air between the two sails during the hoisting and lowering operations, and (5) setting or dousing the sail that is on the *inboard* side.

During an inboard change, the jib to be hoisted or removed is to windward of the other jib, but such a set requires a free windward halyard. For example, if the boat were on the port tack, the jib halyard on the port side should be free. When that halyard is not free but the one to leeward is, it may be advisable to come about if you are short-tacking on a beat to windward. In this case, you would tack to make the proper halyard available for an inboard set and then tack again after the replacement sail is hoisted so the sail to be lowered will be inboard. When tacking is not possible, of course, the somewhat more difficult outboard set will have to be made, and the replacement jib is hoisted to leeward of the jib that is to be lowered.

Another alternative, which may well be advisable in heavy weather or when reaching if the sail to be lowered is outboard, is to set an interim staysail and then lower the jib before hoisting its replacement. The purpose of the staysail is obviously to keep some sail in the foretriangle during the change. There is always some space between the staysail and jibs, so there is no problem with friction.

When one jib is hoisted before the other is lowered, it is important to keep some large pockets of air between the sails to reduce friction. This is not easy, however. One trick is to slack off the halyard of the old jib slightly before the new one is hoisted so that prominent wrinkles along the luff of the old sail will keep the two sails somewhat apart. When lowering a windward jib, its clew and leech should be pulled forward as much as possible to introduce some air between the sails. Turning a foil having fore-and-aft slots may also help.

Double-slotted foil systems also can be modified for roller furling on cruising boats. Conventional roller furling reduces area or furls a headsail by winding it up on its own luff. The jib is sewn on a luff wire that is rotated by pulling on a furling line wound around a drum just below the tack. There are two main problems with the conventional system. First of all, there is nearly always too much luff sag, because, regardless of the mechanical advantage given to the halyard (with purchases or winch size), the luff cannot be made sufficiently taut. Second, it is not always suitable to sail for prolonged periods in heavy weather with a large jib partially furled because of twisting stresses, chafe at the leech and foot against the wound-up sail, and the inefficient shape of the sail. Certain double-slot foils, however, alleviate some of these problems, since most aluminum foil extrusions and the tensions under which they can be carried minimize luff sag. Furthermore, the double slots allow sail changes, so if there is a prolonged period of sailing upwind in heavy weather a smaller, more suitably shaped jib may be used. Conventional roller furling normally makes the changing of headsails a very difficult operation. For extra safety at sea, however, I would prefer the type of foil that fits over the headstay so that there is a backup in the event that the foil should happen to break.

A problem with double-slot roller furling is that sail is more difficult to keep on board when lowering or hoisting if there are no hanks holding the luff. The sail is likely to be partially blown or washed overboard. As mentioned before, lifeline nets forward will help, but for the cruising boat, I would consider the use of luff slugs that fit inside the foil slots and serve the same purpose as hanks (see Figure 2-5). Of course, automatic feeding must be sacrificed with this arrangement, but even a bolt rope may need occasional help into the feeder, and the cruiser is not overly concerned about maximum speed during a sail change.

Handing Sails

Taking in sails, of course, nearly always requires a trip from the cockpit to the mast or foredeck. In heavy weather, especially at night, the crew member going forward should wear a safety harness having a stout lanyard with a heavy snap hook that can be clipped onto some secure part of the boat. Surprisingly, not many American boats seem to be

equipped with jacklines. These are wires or dacron lines running along each side of the cabin trunk. They will accept a
safety lanyard's snap hook and allow continuous movement
along the deck without the need to unclip and then reclip. In
my opinion, they are vital for rough-water offshore work, especially when visibility is poor and in cold weather, at which
times a man going overboard may not have a good chance of
being rescued.

Mainsail halyard reel winches were discussed before, but one
somewhat controversial aspect of their use has not been mentioned thus far. Some seamen insist that the winch handle
should be inserted before lowering the mainsail in order that
the halyard can be eased slowly. When the brake is suddenly
released, the main may come tumbling down rapidly, and it is
possible for the wire to backlash on its reel in much the same
way that a fishing line can backlash. Certain seamen feel that
even with the screw-toggle type of brake release, which allows
gradual easing, the handle should be inserted, because corrosion may cause the brake to release suddenly.

My own feeling, after using a screw-toggle brake for a considerable period of time in the ocean, where it was exposed to
a lot of salt water, is that the winch handle is unnecessary and
can be dangerous. It is always possible for the handle to slip
out of the operator's hand and strike him in the head. As long
as three practices are followed, I think it is preferable not to
use the handle. First of all, occasionally wash off the brake
with fresh water to remove salt deposits that could be harmful
to smooth operation (for obvious reasons never use oil or a
lubricating spray on the brake band). Second, ease the downhaul in order to release luff tension before the sail is lowered.
Third, turn the screw toggle very gradually so that the brake
is eased off, and then let the main come down fairly slowly. If
it starts to descend too fast, the toggle can be tightened a bit.
Regulating the speed of descent is not really difficult if the
winch is kept in good working order.

One rule that applies to lowering a mainsail as well as to
hoisting it is that the boat should be headed up fairly close to
the wind so that the sail will not be blown against the

shrouds and spreaders. Be sure the topping lift is attached and the mainsheet is taut enough to hold the boom fairly steady. In gathering in and muzzling a sail, some sailors grab it at the top of the folds, but this is not correct, for it may cause the sail to balloon due to air getting underneath the folds. The proper method is to grab the lower part of the sail, being careful to keep clear of the battens, and thus spill the wind. Once the sail is muzzled, the leech is pulled up to form a kind of hammock into which folds of slack cloth can be stuffed. A novice will sometimes bend the battens when the mainsail is furled, but they should be pulled aft so that they lie flat (horizontal) before the sail is rolled up. When the main is secured to the boom with slides on a track, rather than a boltrope in a groove, sail stops (or *ties*, as the British call them) should be passed under the foot, then around the sail, and finally under the boom before they are tied.

A common mistake in covering a sail is to wrap the collar and the forward part of the cover around the mast outside the halyards. The cover should go *under* the halyards so that the collar will fit the mast snugly and keep out rainwater. If the collar is outside the halyards, water runs down the mast and soaks the luff of the sail.

As mentioned earlier, a jib is more easily lowered while running, but if it has a long foot the sheet must be eased so that the clew can be pulled inboard. Care must be taken, however, not to slack the sheet so much that the sail will be blown far forward. A frequent problem when one man is lowering and muzzling the jib is his inability to control the halyard. If it is released entirely as the sail is being hauled down, the halyard will often foul. Usually it is best to lead the halyard under its winch and carry it forward, so that the jib can be hauled down with one hand while the halyard is slacked with the other until the sail is mostly down and both hands can be used for muzzling. Of course, the halyard must be neatly coiled so that it can run aloft without fouling. It is sometimes better, especially with braided line, to flake down the halyard using overlapping figure-eight turns (as illustrated in Figure 2-6) just prior to lowering the sail. A stop or two should be

FIGURE 2-6: HALYARD CONTROL

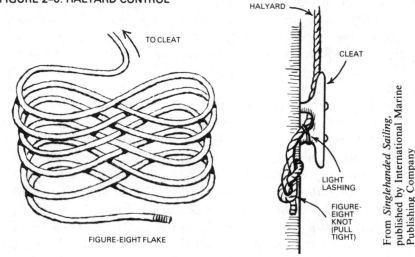

TO CLEAT

FIGURE-EIGHT FLAKE

HALYARD

CLEAT

LIGHT
LASHING

FIGURE-
EIGHT
KNOT
(PULL
TIGHT)

From Singlehanded Sailing, *published by International Marine Publishing Company*

carried in the sail hander's pocket or perhaps tucked under his belt so that the luff can be lashed down at once after the jib is doused.

As mentioned in Chapter 1, it is important to see that the bitter ends of halyards are well secured; otherwise they can go aloft when sail is lowered. Most halyard cleats have holes or openings in their bases, so the halyard end can be run through and secured with a figure-eight knot (see Figure 2-6). It is often a good idea to pull the knot a few inches away from the cleat and permanently lash it to the cleat base with light line as shown in the illustration. This will keep the knot from interfering with cleating and possibly causing a temporary jam. Internal halyards, of course, need stopper knots in their ends to keep them from disappearing into the mast exits. There also should be provisions for securing the shackle end of the jib halyard at the mast and at some point forward such as the bow pulpit or a forward stanchion.

Another method of lowering a jib when short-handed that avoids any need to run off the wind is to lower away with the sail aback. This has the advantage of subduing the sail in a blow and keeping it well inboard. The jib can be backed by hauling in on the windward sheet or tacking without releasing the leeward sheet. With the latter method the sheet may have to be eased somewhat, especially if the sail has a long foot, because otherwise wind pressure might make the lowering operation too difficult. Naturally, you should check that the sail will not become snagged on anything aloft before lowering.

Racing sails may need folding before they are bagged in order to minimize creases and wrinkles. Fold the sail so that the few unavoidable creases run fore and aft horizontally. A cruising sail can be stuffed into the bag, and usually it is put in clew first (or perhaps head first if sheets are left on) with the tack last (as mentioned earlier). It is wise to leave any head and tack pendants attached to the sail. Be sure the bag is amply large, has a sturdy drawstring at its neck, is clearly marked with the name of the sail it holds, and has a heavy strap (for lashing or pulling against) sewn on its bottom.

Taming the Spinnaker

The spinnaker deserves a separate section, because this fast but unseamanlike sail is completely unique and requires special handling techniques. The main difference between a parachute spinnaker (commonly called the 'chute) and more conventional sails is that it is supported by three corners only and has a comparatively deep camber. Thus it can twist, oscillate, fill prematurely, collapse, and wrap its belly around a stay like a boa constrictor. In some of my previous books, especially *Sail and Power* and *The Racing-Cruiser*, I've gone into the various difficulties one can encounter while carrying the spinnaker. Here, I'll concentrate only on the most common problems and those with the most serious consequences.

Hoisting the 'chute in a breeze requires the greatest care, because premature filling can cause a crew member painful rope burns from the halyard running through his hands. To avoid early filling, be sure the 'chute is blanketed behind a large jib while it is going up, and be sure the boat is headed far off the wind. Also, hoist with one turn of the halyard around its winch, and use rope sufficiently thick that it can be firmly gripped. I prefer a laid or twisted line rather than the smoother braided lines that can so easily slip through your hands.

On large boats in strong winds, of course, the spinnaker can be stopped (bunched between its leeches and tied with light twine so that the sail resembles a long, thin sausage). Trimming the sheet will break the stops if they are weak, but if stronger stopping twine is used, a special breaking line will need to be rigged under the stops. A new stopping method is to pull the sail head first through a plastic bucket having its bottom cut out and with a lot of rubber bands around the bucket which can be slid one at a time onto the sail as it is being pulled through (see Figure 2-7, A). A special device for this purpose is the Spinnaker Stop made by the Dwight S. Williams Company, of 40 E. 34th Street, New York, New York 10016.

In recent years, special devices such as the Zip-R-Turtle and Spinnaker Sally have been introduced to assist in setting the 'chute. The former consists of a zipper whose two halves are stitched about a foot apart up the centerline of the sail from the head to a point just above the foot. The part of the sail between the zipper halves forms a tube that holds the bunched body of the sail after the two zipper halves have been closed. The zipper is opened by trimming the sheet, but it must be closed by pulling on the tab with special pliers. Most sailmakers can install the device and supply complete operation instructions.

I have never used a Spinnaker Sally (Figure 2-7, B). It looks complicated, but its manufacturer claims it is very effective not only for setting the 'chute but also for handing it. The device consists of a number of interconnected plastic rings that are carried above the head of the spinnaker when they are not in use. When the sail is to be handed, the rings are pulled down with a special line to encircle and in effect furl the 'chute. Then, of course, the rings are hauled aloft when a set is desired. More information on the device can be obtained from Jack W. Fretwell, Jr., Millwood, Virginia 22646. A somewhat similar device called a Spee-Squeezer is used in England. The 'chute is packed in a long, tube-like nylon sock, the bot-

FIGURE 2-7: MODERN METHODS OF SETTING SPINNAKER

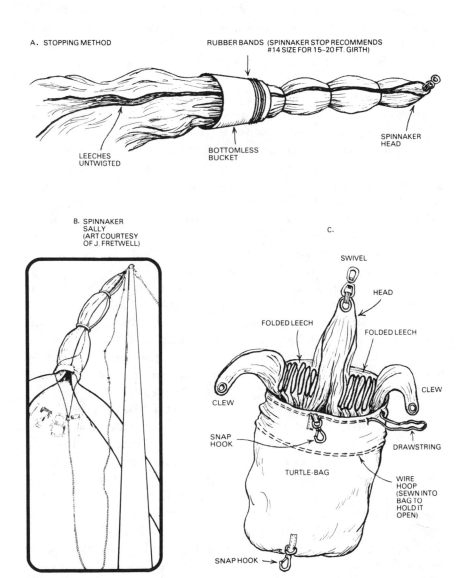

A. STOPPING METHOD

RUBBER BANDS (SPINNAKER STOP RECOMMENDS #14 SIZE FOR 15–20 FT. GIRTH)

SPINNAKER HEAD

LEECHES UNTWISTED

BOTTOMLESS BUCKET

B. SPINNAKER SALLY (ART COURTESY OF J. FRETWELL)

C.

SWIVEL

HEAD

FOLDED LEECH

FOLDED LEECH

CLEW

CLEW

SNAP HOOK

DRAWSTRING

TURTLE-BAG

WIRE HOOP (SEWN INTO BAG TO HOLD IT OPEN)

SNAP HOOK

tom of which is held open by a bell-shaped ring. To set the spinnaker the filled sock is hoisted, and then the bell is pulled aloft, allowing the 'chute to escape. Handing is done by pulling the bell back down, enclosing the 'chute in its sock; then the whole affair can be lowered with little effort. Details can be obtained from Parbury Henty and Company, 44/45 Chancery Lane, London WC2A 1JB, England.

Undoubtedly, one of the most common problems in setting a spinnaker is the hourglass twist. This is often confused with a headstay wrap, because in both cases the spinnaker is pinched in at its middle and balloons above and below the middle; however, the two problems are quite different and must be corrected by different means. The hourglass twist occurs because the leeches are crossed when sail is pulled aloft or the head of the 'chute begins to spin during the hoisting so that a twist occurs near the middle of the sail. To help avoid this predicament, see that the 'chute is properly bagged or turtled, that it is hoisted fast, and that tension is applied at the tack and clew. Of course, stopping the sail and using such setting assists as the Zip-R-Turtle, Spee-Squeezer, and Spinnaker Sally will also help in strong winds.

Before bagging or turtling the 'chute, the leeches must be sorted out and neatly accordion-folded so that they are not crossed and twisted. A usual means of bagging is to fold the leeches side-by-side, working down the sail from the head to a short distance from the foot. Then the two clews are pulled apart, and the loose bulk of the sail is stuffed into the bag followed by the folded leeches. Finally, the three corners of the sail (head and clews) are left hanging a short way out of the top of the bag, and the neck drawstring is pulled taut and tied with a slipknot. Another method that may better assure that there are no twists is to accordion-fold each leech separately and pack them in the bag or turtle separately, a short distance apart (see Figure 2-7, C). It is helpful if the leech tapes are different colors, normally red and green, so a twist can be spotted more easily.

The purpose of hoisting fast is to give the head less opportunity to spin while it is going aloft. Applying tension to the

A 'chute being set with the Spinnaker Sally. Note how the rings contain the 'chute when they are pulled down and how neatly they fit together above the head when the 'chute is fully set. (Photographs courtesy of Jack Fretwell.)

The British Spee-Squeezer system, somewhat similar to the Spinnaker Sally. The Squeezer uses a nylon sleeve and fiberglass bell instead of the interconnected rings that are used with a Sally. (Photograph, Roger M. Smith, courtesy of S. B. Roberts, Parbury Henty and Co., Ltd.)

tack and clew holds the sail open with the leeches apart to help prevent twisting. This means that the guy and especially the sheet should be pulled taut promptly while the sail is being hoisted.

An hourglass twist near the head or even the middle of the sail is usually not difficult to clear. The simplest means is to slack off the halyard a foot or so and give it a few violent jerks. This should cause the swivel at the spinnaker head to turn and the sail to untwist. Tugging on the leeches and foot also may help. A twist near the foot is more difficult to clear, and in fresh winds it may require lowering the sail. In light airs, however, the tack and clew can be detached without lowering, and the bottom of the sail can be unwound. During this operation, it is important to keep the 'chute well blanketed.

A less frequent but more serious predicament is the headstay wrap, in which the deep middle section or belly of the sail wraps around the headstay. The 'chute is especially vulnerable to this difficulty in rough seas and damp air, when the sail collapses against the headstay. The few times I have had this problem, clearing was achieved by jibing and getting the wind on the other side of the sail so that the wrapped portion unwound itself. Some sailors have not been so fortunate, however, and occasionally it is necessary to send a man aloft in a bosun's chair to unwrap the sail. In one case I heard of, the man aloft was wrapped by the 'chute so tightly that he had to cut his way out with a pocket knife.

An interesting article on de-wrapping a spinnaker appeared in the June 1971 issue of *Yachting* magazine ("De-Wrapping The Spinnaker"). The author, C. L. Moore, described a means of unwinding the 'chute by sailing by the lee and then heading up in a series of swoops, with each swoop reducing the wrap by one turn. Before taking any action, however, the author advised that the direction of wrap should be determined so that the boat can be put on the appropriate tack. He suggested as a rule of thumb that clearing a clockwise wrap requires being on or changing to the port tack, while a counterclockwise wrap requires a starboard tack. Next, a jibing preventer line is rigged, and the boat is sailed slightly by the lee until eddies to leeward of the main cause the wrap to begin unwinding, at which time the boat is turned and headed up sharply until she is slightly higher than the original course. This procedure completes the unwinding by one turn. Other turns are unwound by repeating the maneuver.

Of course, everything possible should be done to prevent a spinnaker wrap in the first place. A foolproof measure is to have a jib set, but this is not always possible, because the jib will often blanket the 'chute. Nevertheless, the jib should be set when hoisting and lowering the spinnaker. At other times a phantom jib, more commonly known as a spinnaker net, will serve the same purpose. The net consists of several lines or tapes used to fill the foretriangle, and three different types are illustrated in Figure 2-8. The simplest nets are merely anti-

FIGURE 2–8: SPINNAKER NETS

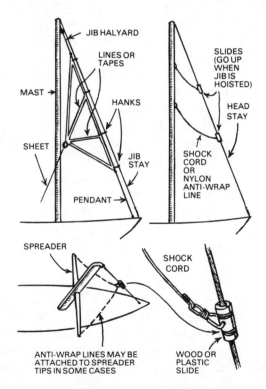

wrap lines, usually of shock cord, permanently rigged from the mast to rings or slides on the headstay. When the jib is hoisted, its top hank carries the rings or slides aloft out of the way of the sail. It should be pointed out that one or two anti-wrap lines are not as effective as the true phantom jib that is hanked to the headstay and hoisted on the jib halyard (see first illustration in Figure 2-8).

Perhaps the spinnaker is most susceptible to a wrap when jibing. Every effort must be taken to keep the sail full and not let it collapse against the headstay, especially when the boat is rolling. Jibing should be well planned in advance and carried out slowly to avoid snafus. A good rule for the sheet and guy trimmers is to keep the chord of the sail (an imaginary straight line from luff to leech) approximately at right angles to the true wind (see Figure 2-9). On medium- to large-sized boats it is usually best to use a dip-pole jibe when the wind is at all fresh, because the pole remains attached to the mast during the entire procedure. Of course, the inboard end of the pole must be at the highest point on the mast in order that the outboard end fitting can be released from the spinnaker tack, swung under the headstay, and reattached to the clew, which becomes the new tack (Figure 2-9). An extra guy or holding line simplifies the task of holding the new tack while the fitting is clipped to the guy. A frequent cause of collapsing the 'chute during a jibe is blanketing from the mainsail. It is usually advisable to keep the main trimmed in a bit and hold it amidships while the 'chute is being jibed. Be cautious about letting the main boom far off until the spinnaker is under complete control.

Reaching with a spinnaker is not the same problem today as it was in former times, before the advent of the specialized reaching 'chute with its flatter draft, narrower shoulders, and corners with radial seams, which minimize bias distortion. Nevertheless, there is a special difficulty with many of the newer boats having inboard shrouds because of excessive compression on the spinnaker pole when it is all the way forward during a close reach. This is because the guy pulls almost directly aft on the pole rather than pulling in a more lateral

FIGURE 2–9: SQUARING THE CHORD
            DURING A JIBE

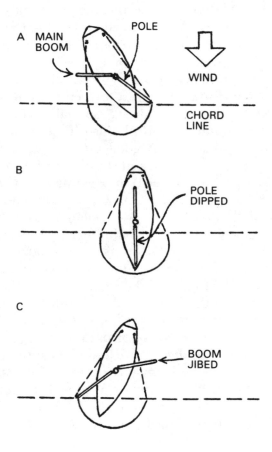

direction, as would be the case if the shrouds were located
further outboard. To counteract this compression a reaching
strut is needed on most relatively new boats. This strut, which
is illustrated in Figure 2-10, attaches to an eye on the mast
and holds the guy several feet outboard of the shrouds. Occasionally a special lift is used for the strut, but this seems to be
an unnecessary complication unless the boat is quite large.
Normally, the strut can be lashed to the shroud (see Figure 2-
10).

FIGURE 2–10: REACHING STRUT

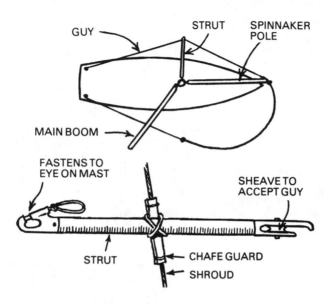

GUY — STRUT — SPINNAKER POLE

MAIN BOOM —→

FASTENS TO EYE ON MAST

SHEAVE TO ACCEPT GUY

STRUT — CHAFE GUARD

SHROUD

A Whitby 45 using the reaching strut. Notice that the angle between the guy and the spinnaker pole is increased by the strut, thereby lessening compression on the pole and strain on the mast. The curling spinnaker luff reveals that the sail is just beyond being "on edge." (Photograph, Joe Fuller.)

The beginning of a broach. This Tartan 41 flying a tri-radial spinnaker is being tested by sailmakers. At the first indication of a broach, a reaching boat should be headed off at once before the rudder begins to stall. A star-cut would give this boat greater stability in these conditions. (Photograph courtesy of Murphy and Nye Sailmakers.)

Modern reaching 'chutes also help alleviate the problem of spinnaker knockdowns, because their flatter draft and resistance to distortion mitigates side force, which causes heeling. However, many modern boats (especially those with shallow spade rudders whose turning axes have considerable forward rake) are susceptible to broaching (inadvertently rounding up into the wind). When struck by a strong gust while reaching with the spinnaker up, it is important to bear off at once before the rudder stalls and loses its effectiveness. Easing the sheet and carrying the pole as far aft as possible is also helpful in preventing a knockdown to leeward. If a knockdown and broach cannot be avoided, however, the sheet should be let right out so that the sail can spill its wind.

It is also possible for the boat to be knocked down to windward when she is running with the 'chute set in a strong wind. This is most likely to occur when the boat is rolling and the 'chute is carried far around to windward with the pole all the way aft and the sheet well eased. To avoid a windward knockdown head higher so that you are broad-reaching, ease the pole further forward, and trim in the sheets. It also will be helpful to keep the mainsail well vanged, because otherwise the sail will twist, causing the upper leech to fall off and exert a force to windward. In conditions that pose a threat of serious knockdowns, of course, it is more seamanlike not to carry a parachute spinnaker. Quite often a boomed-out jib can be carried when running, and it can afford just as much or more speed when the wind is really piping.

Handing a spinnaker is not difficult if the sail is kept blanketed, but quite often racing sailors wait until the last minute when they are rounding a turning mark before lowering; and when the boat is turned, the sail blows aft, away from the lee of the mainsail, and becomes hard to control. Usually, it is much better to lower while headed downwind so that the sail is well blanketed. This will waste little or no time if the turning mark is approached in such a way that the boat can be headed up to fill her jib immediately after the 'chute is doused. Furthermore, any time that has been lost can be compensated for by a smarter rounding with quicker trimming of mainsail and genoa sheets when the boat is turned upwind.

Miscellaneous tips for lowering and handing the spinnaker are as follows:

● Before lowering the 'chute, lower the outboard end of the pole so that it can be reached easily by a man at the bow. Ease the pole all the way forward, but be careful that it doesn't slam against the headstay, especially if the boat has a luff foil that can be dented or cracked.

● Cast off the tack before lowering so that the luff will stream off to leeward and spill wind from the sail.

● At the end of the guy be sure to use a full-release snap shackle that cannot hang up on the tack when the shackle is opened. Also use a sturdy lanyard on the pull pin of the shackle to simplify opening in a strong wind.

● Some sailors release the tack by casting off the guy and letting it run through the pole end. If you use this method, lash or tape the pull pin so that it cannot move, because shackles can be whipped open by a flapping sail. I once lost a guy this way.

● If the sheet should happen to get away from the man tending it after the tack has been released, the spinnaker will fly from the masthead like a flag and be very difficult to retrieve. This can be avoided by putting a knot in the end of the sheet just before taking in the 'chute so that if the sheet escapes it will be stopped when the knot catches in the lead block.

  • Lower the 'chute with one or more turns of the halyard on its winch in a fresh breeze.

  • Lower no faster than the crew handing the sail can take it in, muzzle it, and stuff it below.

  • Hand the 'chute by one leech and the foot only, because pulling on both leeches at once will cause the sail to fill and become very difficult to manage.

  • If the sail should happen to go overboard, haul it back aboard by one corner only; otherwise it will fill with water and pull like a sea anchor.

A relatively new development (for large boats, at least) is the handing of a spinnaker with a retrieving line. This is a line secured to a reinforcing patch in the middle of the 'chute (located a little above center) and leading down to the deck, where it is belayed with considerable slack. It is used to pull the sail down and inboard while the halyard is being eased off. This method of handing is similar to the usual way in that the pole is guyed forward and the 'chute is lowered behind a hoisted jib; but when the retrieving line is used, the tack need not be released initially, since hauling the sail down by its middle will spill the wind, the sail is normally handed under the jib and into the foredeck hatch rather than under the main boom and into the companionway hatch. This is a big advantage for a boat with her sheet and halyard cleats and winches located on the after end of the cabin trunk, because the normal douse into the companionway will often block vision and cause the sail to become entangled with the lines or winches. A disadvantage of the retrieving line, aside from having "another string to pull," is that hauling the sail down by its center will often cause the corners and edges to drag momentarily in the bow wave. However, this should not cause any great harm, because the sail cannot trap water and fill so long as it is being pulled only by its middle.

With the variety of specialized spinnakers now being carried on racing boats, there is greater need of changing these sails for varying conditions. The usual changes are the replacement of a general-purpose working 'chute (normally a three-quarter-ounce radial-head) with a star-cut reacher or a half-ounce floater or vice versa. Quite often these changes can be made most simply with very little waste of time by lowering the original 'chute before hoisting its replacement. When replacing a general-purpose worker with a floater or vice versa, the change is made in near drifting conditions so that a momentary empty foretriangle makes little difference. And with the star-cut change, the course is normally the closest possible spinnaker reach; thus an interim jib may be carried effectively during the change. For the short time the interim jib is hoisted it might be advantageous to point higher and gain distance to windward so that you can crack off a bit for more speed when the new 'chute is hoisted.

Of course, a replacement 'chute can be hoisted before the original one is lowered when the boat is fitted with two halyards. An effective method of doing this is the so-called inside-outside change, in which the replacement 'chute is hoisted to leeward inside the sheet of the original 'chute as illustrated in Figure 2-11. Notice in the illustration that before the replacement sail is attached to the spinnaker pole its tack is held by a short piece of wire secured to the bow pulpit. At the top of the wire is a snap shackle that snaps onto the tack, and in addition there is sometimes a jib hank near the shackle to hold the unit close to the headstay (see Figure 2-11). This gear is often called a changing wire or a Jano strap when the lower end of the wire is led into the pulpit pipe and attached to a length of shock cord to make the wire retractable. After the replacement 'chute has been hoisted, secured, and trimmed as shown in Figure 2-11, the tack of the original 'chute is released by tripping the guy snap shackle, and the sail blows around behind the replacement 'chute. Next, the guy shackle is attached to the new 'chute, the changing wire shackle is tripped, and the old 'chute is lowered and hauled in by its sheet. Meanwhile, the pole is squared and the sheet of the new 'chute is eased. An article and sequence of photographs showing this opera-

FIGURE 2–11: CHANGING SPINNAKERS

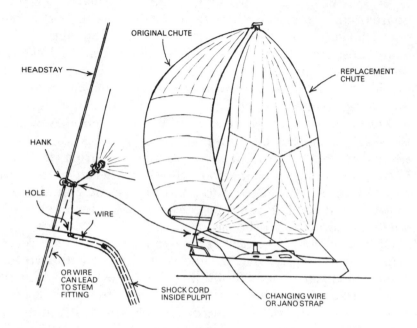

ORIGINAL CHUTE

HEADSTAY

REPLACEMENT CHUTE

HANK

HOLE

← WIRE

OR WIRE CAN LEAD TO STEM FITTING

SHOCK CORD INSIDE PULPIT

CHANGING WIRE OR JANO STRAP

tion appeared in the December 1972 issue of *Yacht Racing* ("Inside-Outside").

A final thought on handling any sails, especially spinnakers, is to double-check the rigging of all lines such as sheets or guys and halyards to see that they are properly led and will not become fouled. Special care must be taken to see that these lines will not become fouled on or under (or chafe on) lifelines, pulpits, or shrouds. By all means look aloft before hoisting or lowering any sail and occasionally while the sail is flying. I was once told that the competence of a seaman can be judged by how often he looks aloft. Certainly it is true that the best seamen are constantly keeping a watchful eye for potential trouble whether it is aloft or alow.

3

Sail Shape and Trim

In recent years, as a result of changing technology, rating rules, and new aerodynamic theory, there has been a subtle revolution in the fine points of shaping and trimming sails. Although basic theory will probably never change radically, minor modifications of former thinking are very much in evidence. Many of these changes are not always easy to understand, especially since sailmakers often differ in their opinions, and as we all know misunderstandings inevitably lead to confusion and errors.

Some of the departures from traditional concepts of sail shape and trim are as follows: (1) sails have higher aspect ratios (they are taller and shorter on the foot); (2) sheeting angles are narrower; (3) the position of maximum draft or camber is further aft; (4) camber is deeper and more uniform from head to foot; (5) traveler slides are often carried to windward; (6) lead positions for jibs and spinnakers are somewhat further forward; (7) greater use is being made of a variety of staysails and other specialized headsails. This modern thinking is in general based on sound concepts, but certain practices are sometimes overdone. It could be said that most of the sail

69

A sloop that exemplifies the older low-aspect rig. There are subtle differences between this type and the newer high-aspect rigs in regard to sail shaping and trim.

shaping errors by modern sailors are a result of either over-reacting to the new theories, or at the other extreme, having too little regard for them.

Shape and Draft Control

High-aspect-ratio sails have been known to be efficient since early times, but their use was discouraged mainly by handicap rating rules and the adverse effect of tall rigs on a boat's stability. Today, however, designers are creating racing boats with greater stability—with more beam and lower centers of gravity (made possible partly by new mast and hull construction materials); and most important, present rating rules, the International Offshore Rule (IOR) in particular, have placed less penalty on rigs with high aspect ratios. The IOR also encourages (or fails to discourage) a large foretriangle (the area between the headstay and mast) and a smaller mainsail. This new look in rigs combined with changed hull configurations (encouraged by the latest rating rules) plus recent technological advances in sailcloth and construction methods, has produced new ideas regarding sail shape and trim.

The position of maximum camber has moved aft in sails primarily because modern sailcloth is more stable and the draft is less prone to move aft as the wind increases. In former times maximum camber had to be further forward because an increasing wind would cause it to blow aft, where it would cause the leech area to form an extreme hook to windward and thus deprive the sail of forward drive while adding to the drag and heeling forces. Another reason for not having the draft forward in an IOR mainsail is mast interference in combination with high aspect ratio. The mast causes wind turbulence over the entire forward area of the sail, and so most of the drive must come from the middle area. In general, it is now recommended that maximum draft in a mainsail be located at a spot between 45 and 50 percent of the chord length abaft the luff (the chord being a straight line between the luff and leech), while for the genoa it should be between 40 and 45 percent aft.

As for the amount of draft, this will depend to some extent on whether the sail is intended for light or heavy winds, but in general the draft is deeper than in previous times. Some reasons are that moderately deep draft produces more power, and when it can be placed further aft there is no loss in pointing ability, since the angle of attack of the wind against the luff remains about the same (Figure 3-1). Furthermore, if the sail can hold a gradually rounded shape, rather than an abruptly curving or distorted shape, there is less chance of its stalling—that is, having the airflow to leeward separate from the sail and cause turbulence that destroys lift.

FIGURE 3-1: MAINSAIL DRAFT

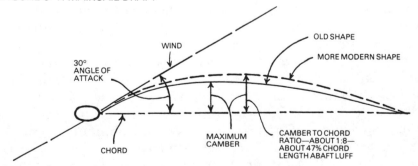

Most sailors know that they can alter draft in various ways for optimum performance under a variety of wind conditions and points of sailing. These methods include increasing or decreasing on the luff and foot, bending the spars, using foot zippers and flattening reefs, adjusting leech lines, and controlling headstay sag. The last, of course, applies only to altering the shape of the jib, and it is probably the most abused method of draft control. Many racing sailors carry the headstay as tight as they can get it all the time, at least when beating to windward. I have been guilty of this practice myself, but it is wrong to have a bar-taut headstay in light airs even when beating, because a bit of sag will put more draft in the sail for added power. Fairly full draft is needed for choppy seas, also, but in this case fullness is best achieved by other methods, because an overly slack stay will jump around too much as the boat pitches. Of course, a very taut headstay is needed when beating in moderate to heavy winds with moderately smooth water, but under these conditions many cruising sailors carry the stay far too loose, and this severely hampers their windward ability. Off the wind some slack is needed to increase draft and power.

One of the most effective means of controlling draft, especially its location fore and aft, is with luff tensioning. A tight luff tends to flatten the sail and move the draft forward, while a slack luff adds draft and moves it aft. Modern sails, usually made with stretchy luff ropes or tapes, are particularly sensitive to luff tensioning, but a great many sailors misuse this valuable control. Common errors are failure to alter tension (slacking the luff in light airs and when reaching in moderate winds and tightening the luff in heavy winds) or else altering to improper tensions. Quite often the luff of a genoa is overtensioned for beating in a fresh breeze with rough seas. An extremely taut luff on a heavy jib made of stable cloth may flatten the sail too much and deprive it of power for getting through the waves; and forcing the draft too far forward may cause premature luffing and thus lessen the ability to point. A North Sails newsletter described sailmaker Art Ellis's participation in the 1974 Ensign Nationals as follows: "In previous

An example of a very poor-setting sail. Although it is doubtful that any kind of adjustment could change the mainsail on NA 2 into a good-looking sail, its shape could definitely be improved by slacking the foot and tensioning the luff. Note that the jib luff is also too slack. (Official U. S. Navy photograph, courtesy of the U. S. Naval Institute.)

A well-trimmed genoa on a Carter three-quarter-tonner. Note that the luff is not stretched excessively tight for this breeze (overtightening is a common mistake). The headstay, however, might be tightened a little more for better windward efficiency. The upper luff yarn is slightly stalled, indicating the need for a bit more twist. This might be achieved by sliding the lead another notch or so further aft. (Photograph courtesy of Murphy and Nye Sailmakers.)

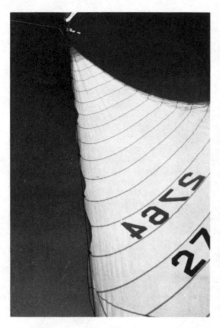

A luff wire that has stretched and is too slack. One can plainly see that tensioning the halyard to remove slack in the wire will crease the luff of the sail and pull the draft much too far forward. This fault was quite easily corrected by a sailmaker. (Photograph, R. C. Henderson.)

A Tartan 41 in a moderate wind with number 1 genoa. Note how the moderately high clew gives considerable overlap without losing the deck sweep forward. Draft in the mainsail has blown aft to form a pocket just forward of the battens. This might be alleviated by bowsing down the Cunningham. (Photograph courtesy of Murphy and Nye Sailmakers.)

heavy air races we had tightened the genoa halyard to bring the draft forward and flatten the genoa, but this time we only tightened it enough to barely remove the scallops between hanks. This gave us a more powerful shape, with the maximum draft at about 45 percent and resulted in a marked improvement in our speed." Of course, a fair amount of luff tension is often necessary to keep the draft from blowing aft, but the adjustment is easily overdone.

On the other hand, the modern mainsail may normally need a bit more luff tension in a fresh wind, because it needs to be quite flat to avoid too much jib backwind (the traveler slide is usually to leeward in a blow), and pulling the draft forward will do little harm, since it will be in the region of mast interference. A very important point is that tensioning the mainsail luff will ease the leech, which is what you want in heavy weather to reduce heeling and excessive weather helm (the tendency of the boat to round up into the wind). Conversely, in light winds you want a fairly tight leech to give the mainsail a full shape and give the boat a better balance for more "feel" on the helm (see Chapter 4); thus the luff should be well slacked.

By the same token, the headsail luff should be slacked in light airs, but this is sometimes overdone. Expert sailmaker and trimmer John Marshall makes the distinction that if the headstay can be slacked in light airs the jib luff should also be well slacked, but if the headstay is not slacked, one must be careful not to ease the luff too much. The maximum camber of the jib should nearly always be a bit further forward than that of the mainsail. By all means mount a scale or put marks on the mast near the halyard cleat and put matching marks (tape or paint) on the halyard to aid in reconstructing luff tension once proper tension has been established through trial-and-error experimentation. Actually, there can be no standard rule for the precise amount that a halyard is tightened or slacked, because the amount will depend on individual cloth weight, finish, and construction and also on how much tension is on the luff rope when it is sewn to the sail.

Cunningham cringles (small reinforced holes just above the tack grommet) are also used to tighten the luff. A line is rove through the cringle and rigged to a tackle or winch to put tension on the luff. The only real advantage a Cunningham adjustment has over tensioning the halyard or downhaul, however, is that it allows the use of a sail with maximum luff length, since the length is normally restricted by the length of the jib stay or by black bands on a mast (required by racing rules when stops are not used on the gooseneck slide and halyard).

To a lesser extent, foot tensioning also controls the draft. Tightening the outhaul tends to flatten the sail and pull the draft down toward the boom, while slacking the outhaul adds to the fullness of the sail and makes it more powerful when beating in light airs or when reaching in wind of any strength. Most modern racing mainsails are built with a con-

FIGURE 3-2: FLATTENING REEF

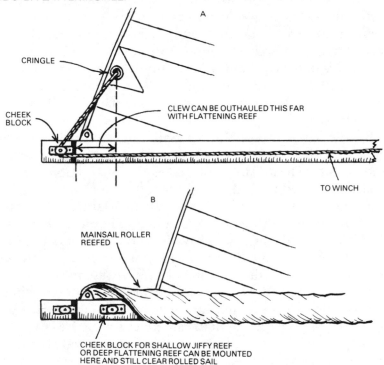

siderable shelf at the foot (with deep draft just above the boom), but the shelf can be closed, reducing draft in that area, with a zipper or with a flattening reef, depending on which system is installed by the sailmaker. The cringle for the flattening reef (see Figure 3-2, A) is perhaps only ten inches or slightly more above the clew, and it serves a purpose similar to that of a Cunningham cringle in that it provides a method of really tightening the foot and folding up the shelf without pulling the clew beyond the black band, which limits foot length, at the outboard end of the boom. The flattening reef is a very useful aid in heavy weather, but it is often omitted from boats equipped with roller reefing, presumably because of the apparent need to mount winches, cleats, and cheek blocks that could damage a sail rolled around them on the boom. In actuality, however, cheek blocks can be mounted aft where they will be clear of the wrapped sail (see Figure 3-2, B), and winches can be mounted forward on the mast. Thus it is perfectly possible to use the flattening reef and then shorten down with roller reefing if the wind gets stronger. Of course, the flattening reef earing must be released from the mast winch before the boom is turned.

The leech line is another sail shaping control that is often not used to full advantage. As a general rule the line should be tightened slightly when beating in light airs and tightened a bit more when reaching. The adjustment helps control the leech area, giving a more rounded draft curve for extra power when the sheets are eased. Furthermore, the leech line helps control the battens on a mainsail with a large roach, and the line is most important for controlling the annoying leech flutter that often occurs on overlapping jibs. Some sailors are reluctant to tighten the leech line on a fluttering jib for fear of cupping the leech and impeding airflow through the slot between mainsail and jib, but a very slight cup does no harm, because it normally lies in a region of moderately turbulent flow; and a bad leech flutter can be harmful by accentuating the turbulence, shaking the whole sail and mast, and distracting the helmsman. Many long-distance cruising sailors would do well to fit their jibs with *heavy* leech and foot lines, not only because of sail shaping control, but also because a constantly fluttering leech or foot can be damaging to the sail on long passages in strong winds.

On small boats, mainsail draft is often effectively controlled with spar bending, especially by bowing the mast. The method is most effective when the jib stay is attached some distance below the masthead, and that part of the mast above the point of attachment is bent aft, while that part of the mast below the point of attachment is bowed forward (see Figure 3-3). Such a bend removes draft from the middle of the sail (for effective beating in fresh winds) but without overly slacking the jib stay. Sailors should be conservative, however, about bending the masts on large boats with masthead rigs. One of the problems is that the large headsail puts enormous stress on a mast out of column, and the bent mast can slack the

The quarter-tonner *Why Why* exhibiting more mast bend than is customary on the normal cruising boat. This bend is made possible by her three-quarter rig, Soling section mast, swept-back spreaders and the fact that her sails are cut for mast bend. (Photograph courtesy of Yacht Yard Sales.)

FIGURE 3–3:
MAST BEND

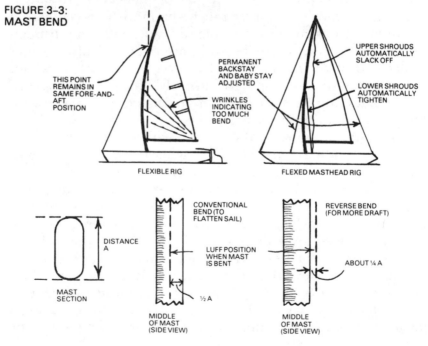

THIS POINT REMAINS IN SAME FORE-AND-AFT POSITION

PERMANENT BACKSTAY AND BABY STAY ADJUSTED

WRINKLES INDICATING TOO MUCH BEND

UPPER SHROUDS AUTOMATICALLY SLACK OFF

LOWER SHROUDS AUTOMATICALLY TIGHTEN

FLEXIBLE RIG

FLEXED MASTHEAD RIG

MAST SECTION

DISTANCE A

CONVENTIONAL BEND (TO FLATTEN SAIL)

LUFF POSITION WHEN MAST IS BENT

½ A

MIDDLE OF MAST (SIDE VIEW)

REVERSE BEND (FOR MORE DRAFT)

ABOUT ¼ A

MIDDLE OF MAST (SIDE VIEW)

upper shrouds while tightening the after lower shrouds, which may cause the masthead to fall off to leeward. Furthermore, spreaders must be designed to accept mast bend, because their tips will tend to be pulled aft as the middle of the mast bows forward. Also, it should be kept in mind that a sail can be distorted by extreme mast bending unless it is specially cut to accept the bend. The usual distortion is revealed by a hard pulled area with wrinkles running from the clew to the middle of the luff as illustrated in Figure 3-3. Nevertheless, a slight amount of mast bowing can be helpful in a fresh-air beat even with a masthead rig. For conservative bending on an offshore boat, John Marshall has given as a rule of thumb a bend that moves the luff forward a distance of one-half the fore-and-aft sectional dimension of the mast (see lower illustrations in Figure 3-3). A very slight reverse bend is also possible, and most sailors, including me, fail to take full advantage of this means of adding draft to the mainsail in light-air reaching conditions.

Of course, this reverse bend, which makes the center of the mast bow aft rather than forward (Figure 3-3), is more difficult to achieve. Conventional bend on a modern racing cruiser is usually accomplished by tightening a short forestay, commonly called the baby stay (see Figure 3-3), and/or tightening the permanent backstay; but reverse bend usually requires slacking the baby stay and permanent backstay while tightening the after lower shrouds (and perhaps setting up on the running backstays if the boat has them). The baby stay is normally controlled with a slide on a track so that adjustment is quite simple, but the after lower shrouds are commonly fitted with turnbuckles having cotter pins that must be removed when adjustments are made. One simple means of lessening this nuisance is to use metal shower curtain rings in lieu of the cotter pins, as suggested earlier. Standard curtain rings can be inserted and removed quickly, but they should be inspected frequently and replaced several times during the season, because sea water corrodes them. Whenever the after lower shrouds are adjusted for reverse bend, of course, a careful note should be made of the amount the turnbuckles are rotated so that they can be returned to their original position when the mast is straightened. I would also caution against the practice of bending the mast in rugged conditions offshore where there is any possible danger of losing the mast.

In comparison with mast bending, boom bending has not been so successful. The reasons are its ineffectiveness in flattening the whole sail and the difficulty of controlling the bend. Quite often when the vang is used on a reach, the middle of the boom will bend down, removing draft from the sail at the very time when draft should be added. I understand that there has been experimentation with wire stays inside the hollow boom to control bend, and so perhaps the method will be improved in the future. Presently, however, I think one is better off with a stiff boom.

A final thought on sail draft control might be directed at the strictly cruising sailor. Methods of changing camber are to some extent restricted by racing or rating rules, but the sailor who never intends to race may have a few effective alternatives not allowed by the rules. For instance, the luff of his mainsail may be reefed or flattened with a curved wire sewn into the sail as illustrated in Figure 3-4, A. Notice that the luff reefing system shown in Figure 3-4, B has a foot Cunningham that is pulled toward the tack in a freshening wind and folds up the luff in much the same way as a flattening reef cringle folds up

FIGURE 3–4:
PRINCIPLES
OF LUFF
REEFING
(FOR CRUISERS)

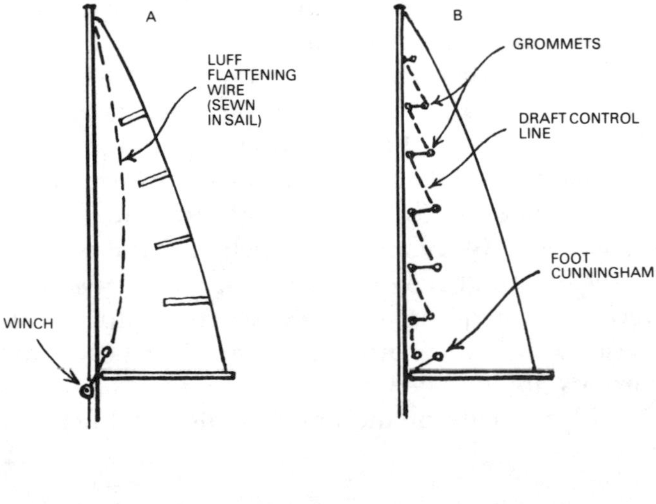

a foot shelf. The lacing then is pulled taut to contain the folded luff. The lacing line and grommets do little harm to the aerodynamic efficiency of the luff, because they lie in the area of mast interference. The luff flattening wire is probably the less desirable system, because when the wire is tightened to remove draft, it puts a great deal of compression strain on the mast, and the wire may add somewhat to furling difficulties when the sail is lowered. I am not necessarily claiming that either method shown in Figure 3-4 is superior to the more conventional methods discussed earlier, but I want to point out that these other options are open to the cruiser. It might be worth noting that some years ago a Cal boat racing in *Yachting* magazine's One-of-a-Kind Regatta had a great success using luff reefing. The system was developed by the sailmaking firm of Baxter and Cicero.

Trim and Twist

In simple terms, the trim of a fore-and-aft sail is its in-and-out position controlled with the sheet. If the sail is out from the centerline of the boat too far, it luffs (flaps at the luff), but if it is trimmed in too close to the centerline the sail stalls; that is to say, the attached flow on the leeward side of the sail separates, forming turbulent eddies that cause loss of lift.

Sailmaker-author Wallace Ross once told me that he considered sailing with the sails partially stalled to be one of the most common mistakes made by sailors, even by many with considerable experience. In former times, neophytes were always trained to sail with the luff on the verge of shaking in order to be assured that the sail was not stalled, but in recent years a better method has come into being—namely, the use of luff yarns. These are usually acrylic yarns or light nylon ribbons taped to or threaded through the luff on each side of the sail. Their principal purpose is to tell the helmsman or trimmer when the sail is stalled by showing turbulence or detached flow on the leeward side, but yarns on the windward side are also helpful in that they telegraph luffing. Theoretically, a sail is properly trimmed when its yarns (or "woollies" as the British call them) are streaming directly aft with a minimum of flutter. Excessive flutter or twirling on the lee side would indicate a stalled condition, while erratic movement and twirling on the windward side would indicate luffing. In actual practice, though, the windward yarn might be allowed to lift above a horizontal position slightly and to flutter just a bit on some boats. More will be said about sailing to luff yarns in Chapter 4.

Opinions differ somewhat on where yarns should be located. Some aerodynamic-minded sailors literally almost cover their sails with yarns, but this practice can be distracting. All that are really needed for steering and basic trimming are three pairs along the luff at high, middle, and low heights (see jib luff yarns in Figure 3-5). The middle-height yarns are the most important, because they are generally near the center of pressure and at a height where the deepest draft is located, but the lowest ones on the jib are important, because they are most easily seen by the helmsman. Upper yarns are especially beneficial in determining twist, which is essentially the difference in trim angles between the upper and lower parts of the sail. Notice in Figure 3-5 that the forward yarns on the jib are near the luff (perhaps a foot abaft the luff rope on a medium-

FIGURE 3-5: BASIC LUFF AND LEECH YARNS

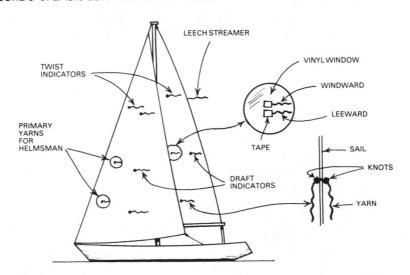

sized boat), but the yarns on the mainsail are further aft, a little forward of the middle of the sail. This is primarily because of the interference of the mast with the flow around the forward part of the mainsail.

Modern sails are usually sufficiently translucent that the leeward luff yarns are visible from the windward side of the sail, but at times the leeward yarns cannot be seen very well due to direct sunlight on the windward side. To solve this problem, small vinyl or similar transparent plastic windows are installed at key locations as shown in Figure 3-5. The kind of window I like is a round one about twelve inches in diameter with two six-inch yarns—a red one taped on the port side of the window and a green one on the starboard side—placed near the center. In this way the yarns can twirl around without getting caught on the stitching of the sail. For the same reason, all yarns should be placed as far as possible away from seams. Some sailors prefer ribbons rather than yarns, but ribbons flutter to a greater extent, and they may be more likely to stick to the sail in wet weather.

Not many sailors use leech yarns, but these can be a help in determining the proper draft and twist. Just a few yarns are shown on or just forward of the leeches in Figure 3-5. When these are twirling but the luff yarns are flying straight aft, they show that the sail has too much camber or that the draft has blown too far aft. The single streamer shown at the mainsail leech tabling is put far aft, because further forward it would be too close to the upper luff yarn. Because the streamer is in the air wake region, it will almost always flutter some, but steadying it down a bit may be useful in determining the best twist and draft. Yarns near the foot of the mainsail are not as helpful, because the flow is nearly always attached when close-hauled due to the overlap of the genoa. On a reach, however, such yarns could be of use.

Although basic trim is primarily controlled with the sheet, twist (or the trim at all levels or heights on the sail) requires additional controls such as changing the position of the sheet leads for the jib and adjusting the traveler and/or boom vang for the mainsail. Of course, the traveler does the job of hold-

A Dutch Contest 29 sporting a rig that looks quite small to the American eye. It is often a mistake to buy a foreign boat with standard rig for areas of the United States where light winds prevail. It is usually not difficult to lengthen the mast by bonding an extra foot or so of mast to a short sleeve fit internally at the joint. (Photograph courtesy of Yacht Yard Sales.)

ing the boom down and away from the centerline of the boat while controlling tension on the leech, and the vang performs the same function on broader reaches (when one has run out of traveler). Incidentally, if your boat is not equipped with a long traveler running athwartships, a vang rigged from the boom to the rail can serve the same purpose, but the arrangement will require coordinated adjustments of sheet and vang. Also, when the boat lacks inboard lead positions for the jib, the so called Barber-haul rig might be used, whereby a second sheet is run from the clew of the jib to a winch mounted on the cockpit coaming, so that the clew can be pulled slightly inboard.

As almost every sailor knows, sheets must be eased out in light airs, especially when seas are sloppy. On modern boats with large foretriangles, the headsail should be trimmed correctly first, and the mainsail should then be positioned to complement the jib. On a light-air beat, the jib leads are brought slightly inboard (if possible) to add fullness and power to the sail, and the lead position is placed further forward to prevent excessive twist, which may result when the sheet is eased. In order to match the mainsail to the jib and keep the slot fairly uniform at all levels, the main boom is brought amidships and some twist in the mainsail is induced by setting the traveler to windward. This is also beneficial in that it minimizes backwind from the added jib camber, and the inboard position of the lower mainsail leech adds a slight amount of feel to the helm.

The usual mistake is to overtrim the sheets, especially the mainsail in light winds. Even though the traveler is carried to windward, the sheet must be started to allow the boom to lift and add some twist to the upper region of the sail. This is important to prevent stalling from overtrim at the top of the sail. Some sailors do not realize that stalling in general is a greater problem in light airs, and the top of the mainsail is a particular problem, because there is no genoa overlap aloft. The only time a vang should be applied on a light-wind beat is when there are sloppy seas (caused by powerboat swells perhaps) and it becomes necessary to hold the boom steady. Vang tension should be very moderate so that it will not remove too much twist. On the other hand, in real drifting conditions when the mainsail simply hangs, it should be flattened to prevent slatting and increase projected area, while the boom is shifted to leeward and held steady with the vang.

Most helmsmen know that it is not wise to pinch a boat in light airs, so they generally sail full-and-by, but this action provides very little benefit unless the sails are trimmed accordingly. In other words, the sheets must be eased until the leeward yarns are attached (streaming aft) when on the full-and-by heading. The harm from overtrim was pointed out in a Charles Ulmer newsletter when sailmaker Charles Wiley wrote of his experience in campaigning a Ranger 33. Concerning his large genoa, Wiley wrote, "Overtrim as little as one inch could cost a half knot in light air conditions." This sounds like a slight exaggeration, but the point is clear.

Overtrimming the headsail is a great temptation on many modern boats, because their shrouds are usually set inboard to allow very flat trim, and they have deck tracks for inboard leads. In some cases provisions are made for sheeting angles of only 6½ degrees. But one should realize that such narrow sheeting angles with flat trim can only rarely be used effectively. You might use them with a fairly narrow slot when beating in moderate winds with very smooth water for high pointing, but in light airs, fresh winds, or anytime seas are bad, you need a wider slot with sufficient draft for power. At times it may be all right to use leads that are far inboard, but the combination of very narrow sheeting angles with flat trim can often be devastating, especially to a heavy boat in light airs.

A very common mistake, of which I have often been guilty, is to overtrim a jib, especially one with considerable overlap, in a strong wind. The sailor often believes that weather helm can be alleviated by slacking the main and strapping in the jib, but this seldom works, because an overtrimmed jib increases heeling, which contributes to weather helm. It is usually far better to ease the jib sheet as well as the main, foot off a bit more, and tighten the jib luff to pull the draft forward and ease the leech.

As the wind freshens on a beat, the genoa lead is moved slightly further aft to open up the slot (because the main is now trimmed on or to leeward to the centerline). Then too, in very fresh winds a genoa lead that is too far forward can put excessive strain on the leech and harm the sail. Also, the jib lead is moved outboard to the rail, which helps open the lower part of the slot and reduce backwind. In the freshening breeze the mainsail traveler is eased to the centerline and then to leeward of center in strong winds to reduce heeling forces in the after part of the sail. Of course, a tight sheet with the traveler to leeward will tighten the leech, but some of this strain can be removed by tensioning the luff, which will also help flatten the sail and keep the draft forward.

The shape of the leech may be judged by looking at the battens. The lower two may be hooked quite a bit to weather in light airs, but in fresh winds they should be closer to parallel with the centerline of the boat. Expert sailor-sailmaker Scott Allen feels that the third batten up is a good indicator of draft and trim. If it hooks to weather it indicates that the sheet is too tight and/or the Cunningham is too loose. Obviously, a tight leech line can make the battens hook to weather also, and the line should only be sufficiently tight in fresh winds to hold the leech reasonably steady (to prevent excessive flutter). Some of these points concerning twist and trim are illustrated.

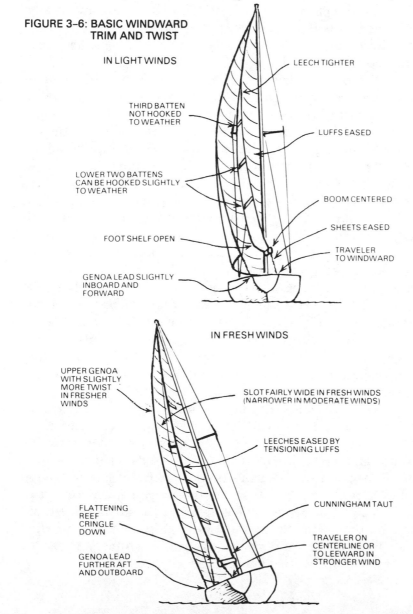

FIGURE 3–6: BASIC WINDWARD TRIM AND TWIST

IN LIGHT WINDS

LEECH TIGHTER

THIRD BATTEN NOT HOOKED TO WEATHER

LUFFS EASED

LOWER TWO BATTENS CAN BE HOOKED SLIGHTLY TO WEATHER

BOOM CENTERED

SHEETS EASED

FOOT SHELF OPEN

TRAVELER TO WINDWARD

GENOA LEAD SLIGHTLY INBOARD AND FORWARD

IN FRESH WINDS

UPPER GENOA WITH SLIGHTLY MORE TWIST IN FRESHER WINDS

SLOT FAIRLY WIDE IN FRESH WINDS (NARROWER IN MODERATE WINDS)

LEECHES EASED BY TENSIONING LUFFS

FLATTENING REEF CRINGLE DOWN

CUNNINGHAM TAUT

TRAVELER ON CENTERLINE OR TO LEEWARD IN STRONGER WIND

GENOA LEAD FURTHER AFT AND OUTBOARD

On the Reach

When reaching, of course, draft is added, and it is moved further aft by reducing luff tension. The traveler is moved all the way to leeward, and the vang should be rigged to hold the boom down, removing excess mainsail twist. In most cases it is also advisable to secure the vang to the rail at a point forward of the boom so that it will hold the mainsail steady, preventing the boom from swinging inboard when the boat pitches in rough seas or powerboat swells. On-center vangs will not do the same job.

The twist of a boomless jib is obviously more difficult to control. Formerly it was most often recommended that the jib leads be moved aft on the reach to increase projected area and open the slot, but such a lead increases the twist of the sail and causes luffing at the head. Today many experts advise moving the lead slightly forward to help remove excess twist. As sailmaker Charles Ulmer wrote me, "It is necessary to move the jib lead forward when reaching with a genoa. This is the only way to keep from losing the head of the sail." Of course, the lead is also moved as far as possible outboard (to the rail) in order to open up the slot and help prevent the leech from hooking to windward.

Sheets are eased out sufficiently far when sailing above the quarter reach to keep the leeward yarns attached. Near the quarter reach, many sailors tend to convert their sails to drag producers rather than keeping them operating as lift producers. We all know that sails operate primarily by drag rather than lift when running, but I think it is a mistake to make the transition too soon. In other words, keep the sheets eased out with the leeward yarns attached as long as possible. The correct time of shifting from lift to drag is most often determined by the particular combination of sails carried. For instance, staysails and/or spinnakers require a flatter-than-normal mainsail trim when the slots become narrow and backwind becomes a problem. By all means have some yarns on *all* of your sails so that you can tell whether each sail is stalled and producing drag with the leeward yarns fluttering or is producing lift with the leeward yarns attached. A properly regulated slot can prolong the use of lift.

One way to combat the genoa twist problem when sheets are started is to set a reaching jib. This sail has a higher clew and a shorter leech than a genoa, and consequently it does not twist off so much aloft. The high clew also allows a greater overlap for a given LP (the length of a perpendicular from the luff intersecting the clew). This is explained in Figure 3-7, A, which compares a reacher and a genoa having the same LPs. Both jibs are 150 percent; that is, their LPs are one and a half times the length of the base of the foretriangle; yet the reacher has more overlap, as shown by the shaded area in the diagram, and the overlapping area is further aloft in better wind. Another benefit of the reacher is that it often allows the effective flying of staysails in the slot for a slight increase in speed.

Modern staysails come in a variety of shapes and names (bikini, banana, chameleon, tallboy, slat, ribbon, windseeker, and so on), but by and large they have higher aspect ratios than those of former times. Not very long ago staysails were regarded as space-fillers beneath high-cut jibs or well-lifted spinnakers; consequently, they were rather low on the hoist and long on the foot. Sailmakers today, however, recognize that most of the thrust comes from the luff; so staysails are made relatively tall and narrow. Some go almost to the masthead, but for versatility on all points of reaching and minimal interference with other sails, a staysail that has a luff length about three-quarters of the mast length and that is tacked down about one-third of the foretriangle base abaft the stem seems to be most effective. Of course, a boat's rigging, particulary the shrouds and spreaders, will dictate the exact shape of the sail. A double-spreader rig with shrouds well inboard will usually have the staysail outside the upper shrouds, but the usual single-spreader rig will most often have the staysail led between the upper shroud and the after lower shroud with the leech almost touching the spreaders for close-hauled work (see Figure 3-7, B).

As compared with a single large genoa, the modern doublehead rig with reaching jib and staysail is nearly always faster when reaching. Some sailmakers even advocate the rig for beating in light airs, but it has definite drawbacks for windward work. Helmsmanship may suffer because the staysail

FIGURE 3–7:
GENERAL–PURPOSE
STAYSAIL AND
REACHING JIB

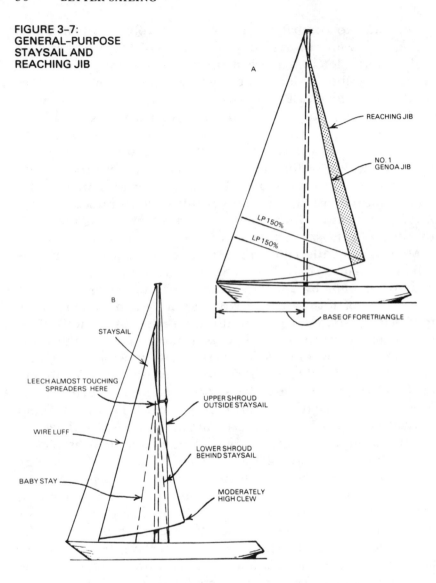

A

REACHING JIB

NO. 1
GENOA JIB

LP 150%

LP 150%

BASE OF FORETRIANGLE

B

STAYSAIL

LEECH ALMOST TOUCHING
SPREADERS HERE

UPPER SHROUD
OUTSIDE STAYSAIL

WIRE LUFF

LOWER SHROUD
BEHIND STAYSAIL

BABY STAY

MODERATELY
HIGH CLEW

blocks the helmsman's view of the jib; the slot is harder to regulate to avoid backwind; tacking is more difficult; and the boat cannot usually point as high as she can with a large genoa. For beating, a specially cut, flatter jib topsail is preferable to a standard reaching jib. The staysail will normally be

An early double-head rig for heavy weather. Light-air double-head rigs use a much larger overlapping jib topsail and a taller staysail. Note the running backstays, which should be set up on the windward side in heavy weather to give the mast support at the point where the forestay joins it. (Photograph, M. E. Warren, courtesy of the U. S. Naval Institute.)

trimmed fairly far inboard of the rail to avoid getting its leech too close to the jib topsail, and the main may have to be trimmed flatter with the traveler set well to windward to avoid backwind from the staysail. The high-clewed topsail must be trimmed quite far aft, but it is a mistake to lead it too far aft, because that will flatten the foot and bring it too close to the staysail. The upwind double-head rig may pay under special circumstances: when the boat is relatively heavy, when she is a footer rather than a pointer, when her overlap is limited by rating or hull form, when she has a highly trained crew, and when she sails windward legs that do not require a lot of short tacks. But for the usual round-the-buoys type of racing with a pickup crew and without restrictions on headsail overlap, I think a single-head rig consisting of a lightweight, moderately high-clewed genoa is the superior arrangement on the light-air beat. Reaching, however, is a different matter. One should nearly always shift to a reaching jib and staysail unless, perhaps, the leg is very short and the sails cannot be changed quickly. As the boat bears away from the wind, the reaching double-head rig is carried until one can set a close-

Sailmakers testing spinnakers on sister three-quarter-tonners. The 'chute on the dark-hulled boat is a tri-radial, while the other is a star-cut. Notice the narrow shoulders and flatter shape of the star-cut, which is intended for closer reaching. (Photograph courtesy of Murphy and Nye Sailmakers.)

reaching spinnaker. This change of sails might be made when the apparent wind angle is about 50 degrees or slightly further forward; but of course the exact angle will depend on the type of boat, the particular sails, the strength of the wind, and other factors.

Under Spinnaker

As with other sails there have been significant advances in spinnaker design. This sail, which formerly could be carried effectively only when the wind was quite far aft, can now be carried when sailing considerably higher than the beam reach. This has been made possible partly because of improvements in nylon sailcloth but especially because of better construction methods. Sailmakers Ken Rose and Bruce Banks of England are credited with developing the so-called star-cut concept, which minimizes bias distortion with the use of radial seams at all three corners of the sail (see Figure 3-8). Radial-heads (sails with radiating seams at the head) have been used with great effectiveness for some time. But if this type of 'chute has its lower half crosscut (in other words, if the lower part has horizontal seams) the sail will stretch out of shape when reaching high in fresh winds. Star-cuts, however, with their radial clews, take the loads approximately in the direction of the weave of the cloth rather than on the bias (diagonally to the weave), and thus the built-in shape is better preserved. Early cruiser star-cuts were nearly always quite small, were cut very flat, and had narrow shoulders. They were specialized sails for high reaching and for running in strong winds, but now radial corners are being used on full-sized, deeper draft, downwind crosscut 'chutes to improve their versatility—that is to give them greater reaching ability without hurting their running performance. This sail is sometimes called a tri-radial or a maximum star-cut (see Figure 3-8).

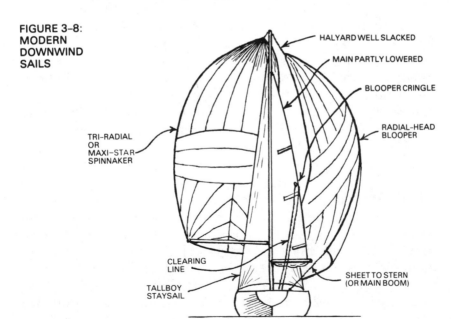

**FIGURE 3-8:
MODERN
DOWNWIND
SAILS**

HALYARD WELL SLACKED

MAIN PARTLY LOWERED

BLOOPER CRINGLE

RADIAL-HEAD
BLOOPER

TRI-RADIAL
OR
MAXI-STAR
SPINNAKER

CLEARING
LINE

SHEET TO STERN
(OR MAIN BOOM)

TALLBOY
STAYSAIL

A Morgan three-quarter-ton boat flying a tri-radial spinnaker. On a reach some beamy boats with inboard shrouds can avoid the use of a reaching strut in moderate weather by leading the guy forward to the rail as shown. (Photograph courtesy of Murphy and Nye Sailmakers.)

The basic rules for spinnaker trim are well known, but some sailors are not so familiar with the exceptions to the rules and many of the finer points. Basics are: keep the pole squared to the apparent wind, the clews level, the pole horizontal, and the pole high except in light airs, and ease the halyard in fresh winds. It is a mistake, however, to adhere blindly to these rules under all conditions and circumstances. For instance, the pole should not (and indeed cannot) always be kept square, at 90 degrees to the apparent wind. In light winds when running it often pays to oversquare it (pull the pole further aft) so that the 'chute has maximum exposure and is not partially behind the mainsail. If sailing dead downwind, even more exposure can be obtained by heeling the boat to windward and thus causing gravity to swing the upper part of the sail to windward. On the other hand, it often pays to undersquare the pole (let it go a little further forward of being squared) in a fresh wind so that the chord of the spinnaker will be more at right angles to the direction of movement of

the boat for the most effective use of thrust and also to prevent
a knockdown to windward during strong gusts (see Figure 3-
9).

The rule for keeping the pole level is a good one, because
this allows use of its maximum length, but on some occasions
the pole should be cocked up or down slightly. In fresh winds
it is desirable to balance the strain on the pole lift and downhaul (foreguy). When the pole is horizontal there is often
greater strain on the pole lift and a tendency for the pole end
to be pulled down by the afterguy (see position *B* in Figure 3-
10). On the other hand, in strong winds there is often a tendency for the spinnaker to "sky" upward, which puts extra
tension on the downhaul, and so the best general compromise
position in gusty winds is with the outboard end of the pole
slightly higher than the inboard end as shown in position *A*,
Figure 3-10. In light airs the pole should be lowered, because
that tightens the leeches and deepens the draft (Figure 3-11).
Cocking the pole downward as illustrated has the same effect
as shortening the pole length; but it reduces the angular slope of
the luff, thus giving it greater resistance to collapsing from the
force of gravity.

FIGURE 3-9: SPINNAKER THRUST ALIGNMENT

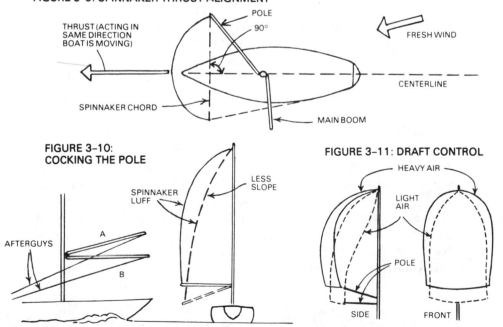

FIGURE 3-10:
COCKING THE POLE

FIGURE 3-11: DRAFT CONTROL

The pole height rule generally holds true, but exceptions occur under special conditions. In fresh winds the spinnaker will tend to lift upward. It should be encouraged to do so, but not to such an extent that a large portion of the head will be horizontal, for this condition will cause the sail to lose too much projected area. To some extent the point of sailing will determine pole height, because running requires a relatively deep camber, while reaching requires flatter camber with more open leeches. As can be seen in Figure 3-11, camber is lessened by raising the pole and increased by lowering the pole. Thus one has to be careful not to raise the pole too high on a run. The close reach in moderate wind requires a fairly high pole for the conventional all-purpose 'chute in order to flatten it and open the leeches, but the flatter-shaped reaching star-cut needs a much lower pole setting, partly to prevent the luff from sagging off excessively and decreasing the ability to point. Bruce Banks has written that a low pole setting with the tack lower than the clew gives the star-cut a highly efficient full-luff, flat-leech shape for very close reaching in light airs.

Draft is also changed to some extent by altering the lead position of the sheet. Bringing the clew near the tack deepens the camber, while spreading the clew and tack decreases camber. With a lead position far aft, altering draft (increasing it for the run and flattening it for the reach) is quite automatic, since the tack-to-clew distance is narrow when running but wide when reaching due to the shape of the boat. However, the problem with a lead located all the way aft is that it tends to flatten only the foot of the sail. This condition is especially undesirable when reaching in fresh winds, because it increases heeling. Then, too, the sterns on modern IOR boats are usually narrow, and a lead far aft tends to hook the leech to windward, causing drag and heeling. When running many of the new broad-shouldered 'chutes will sky upward and lose projected area, thus a more forward sheet lead will help hold the sail down. Most of today's sailmakers seem to feel that the traditional lead to the stern is wrong for new boats with modern 'chutes.

A radial-head spinnaker on a Carter-designed three-quarter-ton boat illustrating how the modern broad-shouldered 'chute will sky upward when broad-reaching or running. To keep the sail from losing too much projected area, the pole is not pushed to the top of its mast track and the sheet is led fairly far forward. (Photograph courtesy of Murphy and Nye Sailmakers.)

Sailmaker Ken Rose, a pioneer in the development of star-cuts, has suggested a method for determining the proper lead position for a reaching spinnaker. It is illustrated in Figure 3-12. On a calm day the spinnaker is fully hoisted, and its tack is held directly over the stem, while the foot, leech, and luff are stretched tight. The sheet is then pulled down and aft at about 25 degrees to a line parallel to the waterline (the rail can be the line if it is horizontal), and the point at which the sheet crosses the rail marks the lead position. Rose admits that the exact position will depend to some extent on the cut of the spinnaker, and he says that the position requires a low pole setting in order to open up the after leech. Perhaps we should not be dogmatic about such a position, but at least it gives a good starting point from which to vary the lead through trial and error. The main purpose of a more forward lead is to induce draft at the foot and keep the camber more uniform at all heights.

When running dead before the wind, the lead can be moved

FIGURE 3–12: METHOD SUGGESTED BY KEN ROSE
(DESIGNER OF STAR-CUT) TO DETERMINE SPINNAKER
LEAD ON A CLOSE REACH

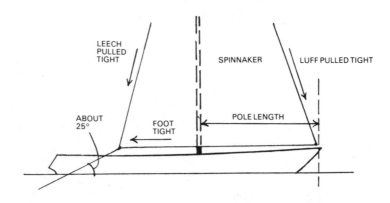

ever further forward. Sailmaker Bob Barton recommends (and has had considerable success with) an extreme forward and inboard lead on the dead run in very light airs. I have noticed (from a nearby boat) Bill Luders, expert sailor and designer, using this same kind of trim. Telltale yarns on the spinnaker are of limited value on a dead run, because the flow to leeward is very turbulent, but on a reach, of course, the flow moves from luff to leech, and then yarns near both edges can be a real help in achieving optimum trim and draft. A useful trick, by the way, is to put a telltale on the middle of the spinnaker pole to help show when the pole is squared to the wind.

Perhaps the most common mistake in using the new spinnakers is trying to carry them too close to the wind. Star-cuts especially can be misleading, because it is possible to carry them on very tight reaches without their breaking but also without their producing the speed of a proper double-head rig. When changing from jib to spinnaker or vice versa, it is very important to compare your speed with that of other boats close by and to keep a careful eye out for changes in the speedometer.

The reaching staysail, one having a long luff and a moderately long foot, can often be carried very effectively under a spinnaker when the wind is not too far aft. On a near beam

The modern high-aspect-ratio rig with its very short main boom on a North Star 26. Notice that the large jib is being carried successfully under the spinnaker, although the jib sheet might be led under the lifeline to avoid chafe. Quite often it is a mistake to lower the jib too soon after the 'chute is hoisted. It may be better to wait and see whether both headsails can be carried effectively simultaneously. (Photograph courtesy of Yacht Yard Sales.)

A handsome yawl in full dress. The staysail is an old-fashioned type designed to fill in the gap beneath the 'chute. Modern reaching staysails are high-lift types with longer luffs and higher clews. Flexible battens in the mizzen would improve the shape of the sail.

A Hughes 38 carrying a tall-boy staysail. This is a marginal sail but one that may in effect augment a short-footed mainsail when running and alleviate mast wake turbulence in certain reaching conditions. Notice the battens, which help control the leech of the staysail. (Photograph, Joe Fuller.)

reach, the staysail can be very large (even a full-size genoa can sometimes be helpful), but on the run, reaching staysails often do more harm than good. If the wind is fresh, over eight knots perhaps, the modern running staysail, commonly called a tall-boy, is of marginal value. This sail, which is tall but has a very short foot, is generally tacked down to the windward rail about halfway between the mast and stem (see Figure 3-8). The function of such a sail, in theory at least, is to augment the area of a high-aspect-ratio mainsail with minimal interference to the spinnaker and improve the flow through the slot.

One value of a spinnaker staysail, often unappreciated, is that it can help prevent broaching on heavy-air reaches. The conventional deep-draft spinnaker with a tight foot encourages the air to flow upward when the boat is heeled on a reach, but a staysail or even a small genoa can help block this flow, which is so harmful to stability. In addition, of course, the extra area forward of the boat's turning axis may help prevent weather helm as long as it does not add significantly to the heeling moment.

A blooper and tri-radial spinnaker on a three-quarter-rigged, quarter-ton racing-cruiser. Notice that the blooper is set outboard of the spinnaker sheet with the halyard well eased to help get it from behind the lee of the mainsail. With this rig, the main is not partially lowered because it supplies as much power as the blooper or more. (Photograph courtesy of Yacht Yard Sales.)

A somewhat controversial but relatively common modern sail that is carried with a spinnaker is the so-called streaker, shooter, or blooper (why can't the new sails have more dignified names?). The sail was conceived as a running nylon genoa set to leeward of the 'chute (outside the spinnaker sheet) for the primary purpose of counteracting the deficiency of the small area and short foot of the IOR mainsail when sailing before the wind. Figure 3-8 shows the way the blooper is normally set, with the halyard well slacked, the tack close to the stem but outside the pulpit and spinnaker sheet, and the high clew trimmed to the stern or possibly the end of the main boom. Notice that the mainsail is partially lowered so that its blanketing will be minimal. Originally, the blooper was a more symmetrical sail, as illustrated by the old shape in Figure 3-13, but in 1974 the rules governing the sail were

FIGURE 3-13: OLD AND NEW SHAPES FOR BLOOPERS

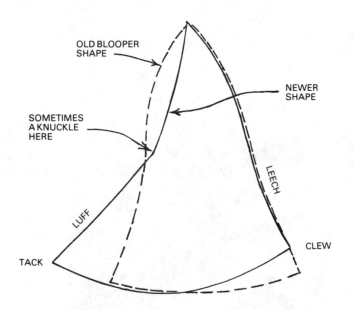

changed, and sails of the new shape, also illustrated, are most often used now. Bloopers are often considered marginal, but they do add considerably to the total sail area, and they may be beneficial at times in balancing the boat downwind by placing more area to leeward where it was formerly located before boats had such short main booms.

One unseamanlike aspect of carrying a blooper with the mainsail down is that the main will be difficult to hoist again because of its being blown against the shrouds and spreaders. A partial solution is to have a cringle in the leech of the main near the next to top batten through which a line is rove to pull the leech away from the rigging as the sail is being hoisted. This clearing line (see Figure 3-8) is doubled, and you haul on both ends when clearing. After the main is hoisted, one end is pulled to remove the line.

A few sailmakers claim that a drifter (a lightweight reaching jib) flown with the halyard slacked makes a reasonably good substitute for a blooper. I think that this is certainly worth a try in the interest of saving money and stowage space, and in the interest of having a more versatile sail that can be used in a greater variety of conditions. However, a specialized sail is usually best doing the specific job for which it was designed.

A final suggestion on sail shaping and trimming in general is that adjustments should be made constantly to achieve the optimum benefits. The wind and heading are constantly changing, and the sails must conform. Headsails are kept on edge, and normally the spinnaker is trimmed so that a very slight roll occurs at the leading edge somewhat above the middle of the sail. In general, the genoa sheet is trimmed in when the wind freshens but eased out during the lulls so that it remains about the same distance—say three to eight inches—away from the spreader tips. Many sailors neglect the mainsail. It doesn't have to be trimmed as frequently as the headsails, perhaps, but it also must conform to and always work with the other sails. On a racing boat, the sheets are not the only adjustments that must be made constantly. The guy, vang, Cunninghams, outhauls, leech lines, traveler, leads, and so on all need continual attention to achieve the optimum shape, twist, and camber. Of course, the adjustments will be far less frequent on a cruising boat, because the cruiser is not so concerned with the greatest possible speed at all times. Nevertheless, all enthusiastic sailors are interested in reasonable performance, and such performance requires frequent if not constant changes in sail shape and trim.

4

Helmsmanship

The famous scientist-sailor C.A. Marchaj, who is generally recognized as being the leading modern authority on sailing aerodynamics, has made the alarming statement that "a first-class helmsman will only once in ten times achieve optimum performance to windward." This statement was not a result of mere guesswork but of conclusions drawn from scientific tests performed under a variety of wind conditions and using a talented helmsman on the 5.5-meter boat *Yeoman*, which was fitted with highly accurate instrumentation to measure her performance. Marchaj was careful to explain that the high percentage of time when a yacht is not sailing at her optimum is not due entirely to deficient helmsmanship, but also to varying wind directions and velocities that make ideal performance "virtually impossible." He wrote, "There must be some time lag between the movement of the yacht off course and correcting action being taken by the helmsman, and this means a decrease in close-hauled performance." Marchaj's conclusion is verified by comparison of human performance with that of an efficient self-steering vane gear sailing a well-balanced boat to windward. The vane will respond more

FIGURE 4–1: EXAMPLE OF WIND OSCILLATIONS
(SOUTHERLY 6–8 KNOTS)

EAST	2 PTS.	1 PT.	SOUTH	1 PT.	2 PTS.	WEST
			8 secs.			
				3 secs.		
			8 secs.			
				11 secs.		
			RAPID OSCILLATION			
			3 secs.			
			RAPID OSCILLATION			
					20 secs.	
				10 secs.		
					60 secs.	
		7 secs.				
			30 secs.			
		RAPID OSCILLATION				
			43 secs.			
				17 secs.		
					11 secs.	
			RAPID OSCILLATION			
			34 secs.			
					9 secs.	
				7 secs.		
					18 secs.	

quickly than a helmsman to wind shifts, and quite often the boat will work upwind more effectively if her helm is untouched by human hands.

Even in the steadiest of winds one finds almost constant minor shifts or brief fluctuations in direction. As an example, Figure 4-1 shows the typical fluctuations of a six- to eight-knot southerly, one of the steadiest winds in my sailing area. The numbers on the chart indicate the length of time in seconds for which the wind held reasonably steady from the south or directions on either side of south. Of course, the chart shows the fluctuations only within one particular brief period of time, and this is merely a random selection from many plots I've made during hours of watching and timing a wind direction indicator; nevertheless, the figure serves well as an example of the wind's lack of steadiness.

Four major causes contribute to this directional unsteadiness: (1) shifting can be due to changes in the general weather system; (2) oscillations can be due to different winds aloft dropping down to the surface of the water; (3) oscillations or shifts can be due to the effect of nearby land, which creates uneven heating, friction, channeling, and so on; and (4) apparent shifts can be due to changes in wind velocity. The fourth case is illustrated by Figure 4-2, which shows what happens when a boat is struck by a puff or a sudden gust. The apparent wind, of course, is the resultant of a vector between the true wind and the breeze caused by the forward movement of the boat as shown in the diagram. During a lull in wind strength the boat speed and true wind will be more nearly equal than during a puff; therefore the gust will cause the apparent wind to draw further aft. This is the reason that boats beating to windward are very often lifted by a puff (provided the puff is not a header that has dropped down to the surface from aloft). Of course, some gusts fan out to some extent so that the boat is headed at first momentarily, but then she is lifted.

Another significant effect on helmsmanship of varying wind speed and direction is the resulting changes in angle of heel. Helm balance of the average boat will change as her heeling increases or decreases. This is mainly due to the fact that the center of effort of the sail moves outboard and thus does not align with the center of resistance of the boat when she heels (see Figure 4-3). Then, too, many modern yachts, especially

FIGURE 4–2:
EFFECT OF A PUFF ON APPARENT WIND

FIGURE 4–3:
TURNING MOMENT
PRODUCED BY HEEL

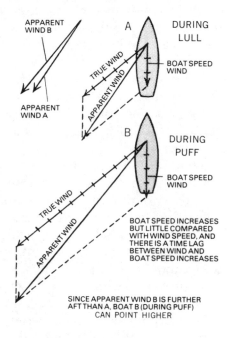

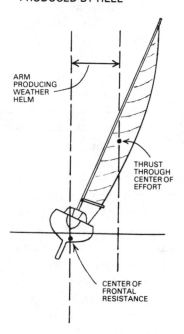

beamy centerboarders or those designed to the IOR, have waterlines that become very asymmetrical with heeling. In other words, the submerged part of the boat to leeward of her centerline is quite different from the submerged part to windward, and this will change the balance.

In addition to the constantly varying conditions of the wind that make it difficult for the helmsman, there is the problem of rough seas. A steep wave taken at the wrong angle when beating or especially when tacking can stop a boat almost dead. The most difficult time perhaps is when a fresh wind has recently subsided but the water is still rough.

With the wind and sea so continually fluctuating, it is easy to see why even a skilled helmsman operates at a low level of efficiency. Can he ever overcome such handicaps? The answer is that he never can entirely. Perhaps he can only aim for about 20 percent efficiency rather than the 10 percent mentioned by Marchaj. However, I think it is reasonable to assume that with proper effort most helmsmen can definitely improve.

Balance and the Helm

The first consideration in an attempt to improve steering efficiency is the achievement of optimal helm balance and the best possible mechanical functioning of the steering system. A great many modern boats very often carry too much weather helm. Sometimes this is unavoidable, but many times the balance can be improved by carrying the right sails correctly trimmed and by proper tuning. A very moderate weather helm is possibly desirable on a boat that has a keel trim tab or a rudder attached to the trailing edge of the keel. In either case the keel might be given some additional hydrodynamic lift as the trim tab or rudder, in effect, creates camber in much the same way that flaps on a wing give lift to an airplane. However, many designers are now coming to the conclusion that keel flaps (trim tabs) or keel-attached rudders that are kept turned to produce lift are actually doing more harm than good because they create a high proportion of drag to lift. Certainly boats with rudders detached from the keel and located at the extreme after end of the waterline should not carry much weather helm, because such a rudder is not giving the keel more lift through the camber effect. This is especially true for a thin, sharp-edged spade rudder that is balanced (having the turning axis abaft the leading edge), because this rudder can stall quite easily and also cause additional drag by its forward edge being to windward of the centerline when the helm is turned to correct for weather helm. On the other hand, a modern boat with a very short keel and a deep skeg-attached rudder may need a little more weather helm in light airs so that lateral pressure on the rudder can be added to the side force produced by the keel and so that the helm will have some feel.

No specific rule can be given for ideal balance, because that will vary with the particular boat and weather conditions. However, a good starting point is to strive for a very moderate and consistent weather helm on a modern, high-performance boat when beating in a ten- to twelve-knot wind. Variations from this norm should be made only after trial-and-error experimentations that involve meticulous monitoring of the speedometer and close attention to pointing ability.

An excessive weather helm, the usual fault, can be corrected or alleviated with the following changes: reducing heel (by adding ballast, moving crew weight aft and as far as possible to windward, and reducing sail); using more effective sails that can be adjusted to move the draft forward and flatten the leech area (refer to Chapter 3); raking the mast forward and/or distributing the sail area so that the total center of effort is farther forward; and, of course, easing the sheets of the after sails. Obviously, the opposite actions will help correct a lee helm. Extremely faulty balance may call for more drastic measures, such as modifying the boat's underbody, extending her skeg, or changing the shape of the rudder. Needless to say, such changes should be made only as a last resort and with the advice of a naval architect.

As for the mechanical functioning of the helm, everything possible should be done to assure ease of operation and optimal response. A great many boats I have sailed have had either too much friction or too much play in their helms. These faults are most discouraging to really sensitive helmsmanship. In many cases, rectification is very simple. Usually lubrication will reduce friction, and tightening nuts at the rudder head fitting or perhaps at the tiller extension will remove excessive play. Occasionally, however, the rudder may be binding against the hull, the fairing, or at the heel as a result of worn bearings, a warped rudder, bent fairing, fiberglass blisters or for some other reason.

For a well-balanced racing boat there is little doubt that tiller rather than wheel steering is more efficient. The tiller gives more instant response and allows a more sensitive feel— that is, the transmission to the helm of varying water pressures on the rudder. It is surprising to see that a great number of racing skippers have their boats fitted with wheels. Although the size and weight of the vessel have a great bearing on whether or not she should be equipped with a wheel, Paul

Elvstrom, whom some observers have called the world's greatest helmsman, has said that he "would steer any boat with a tiller." Evidently he was not exaggerating, for he converted the twelve-meter *Constellation* to tiller steering. For cruising, however, wheels on large boats make sense. They give a mechanical advantage, afford more room in the cockpit when underway, and usually allow more flexibility in placement. Also, the pedestal type affords a handy place for the binnacle close to and directly forward of the helm. Proper maintenance will obviously help the responsiveness of a wheel. Worm gears and cable sheaves must be well lubricated, and it is important to keep the proper tension (minimal slackness) in steering cables. Mechanical advantage should be reduced to the minimum in the interest of obtaining feel and the quickest possible response. I don't care for hydraulic steering, primarily because of its almost complete lack of feel.

Upwind
Once the boat is tuned for proper balance and optimal helm operation, the helmsman can concentrate on his steering. To my way of thinking there are few challenges so stimulating as beating a smart sailing boat to windward; yet doing it well is difficult for the reasons already mentioned. Many helmsmen allow themselves to be distracted and either fall off the wind too far, handle the helm too roughly, or pinch the boat. Doing your best will take complete concentration. One of my worst faults while racing (and I think this holds true for many skippers) is not delegating enough responsibility. There should be a tactician-navigator in the crew who can keep a lookout and tell the helmsman where the other boats are, the location of the windward mark, where the most wind is and whether it is shifting, and so forth. Furthermore, there should be a skilled, attentive sail trimmer so that the helmsman can concentrate entirely on steering. On long races there should be several competent helmsmen, because after several hours or less of steering one man can lose his concentration. Of course, this requires great effort in acquiring, training, and practicing with regular crew members.

More than a few visual aids to helmsmanship are well

known to most racing skippers. They often are not used by cruising sailors, and sometimes they are used improperly or not to full advantage by racers. A case in point is wind direction indicators. I know several cruising men who do not even use simple shroud telltales. One claims that he can tell the wind direction from his masthead burgee, but the burgee is a poor indicator in anything but a fresh breeze, and furthermore, even a proper windsock or counterbalanced vane at the masthead requires considerable bending of one's neck, especially when the helm is forward. This may cause fatigue or even a stiff neck in time. Then, too, constantly gazing so far aloft draws the helmsman's eyes away from more important areas lower down that he should be watching, such as the sail luffs, water, instruments, and so forth. The electronic apparent wind indicator (AWI) is a handy means of watching a masthead indicator without the need of looking aloft, because the wind direction is indicated on a dial at or near the deck

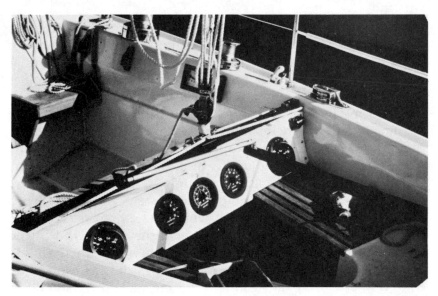

One solution to the problem of where to mount instrument indicators. Mounting instruments beneath the traveler on this IOR racer forces the helmsman to lower his eyes, but the instruments are easily read and they are less blinding in the low location when sailing at night. The square instrument on the side of the cockpit behind the mainsheet is an inclinometer to measure fore-and-aft trim. Hull trim is a consideration that does not always get the attention it deserves. (Photograph, R. C. Henderson.)

FIGURE 4–4: WIND DIRECTION INDICATORS

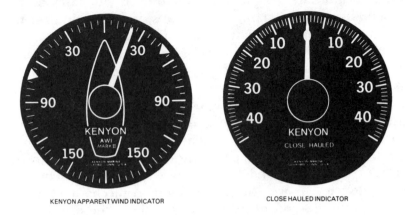

KENYON APPARENT WIND INDICATOR

CLOSE HAULED INDICATOR

Courtesy of Kenyon Marine

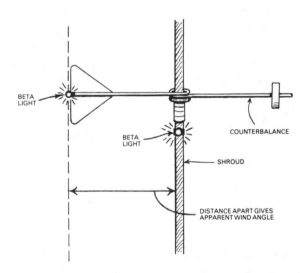

level (see Figure 4-4). Some racing skippers, however, make the mistake of watching this instrument too much. They seem to be almost hypnotized by the pointer and stare at it to the exclusion of other important visual aids. I know one skipper, for instance, who had always been a fairly good light-air helmsman until he bought a boat fitted with an apparent wind indicator. In near drifting conditions he stares at the indicator instead of looking at his sails and the wind on the water, and his boat speed suffers accordingly.

The electronic AWI has certain advantages over shroud tell-tales, such as showing a precise wind angle, having an expanded closehauled indicator (see Figure 4-4), having damping arrangements to inhibit wild swinging when the boat is rolling, and so forth; but the real value is that an indicator with an illuminated dial is a great help for sailing at night. Obviously, telltales are difficult if not impossible to see in the dark. On the other hand, telltales are considerably cheaper, use no electrical power, are not subject to mechanical or adjustment failures, add no weight aloft, show the direction of the wind near the level of the center of effort of the sail (wind velocity is often stronger aloft), and can be placed within or very close to the helmsman's primary field of vision—near the sail luffs. The latter advantage simply means that the helmsman can watch his sail luffs and get a peripheral view of the telltale without shifting his eyes. Whether or not your boat is fitted with an AWI, there is no excuse for not having shroud telltales, since they can be nothing more elaborate than pieces of yarn or ribbon tied as high as one can reach on the outboard and also perhaps on the inboard shrouds. As for the problem of not being able to see telltales at night, I don't see why Beta lights could not be used in the manner illustrated in Figure 4-4. Beta lights are durable, require no battery power or maintenance, and are said to have a life of about fifteen years. They are now made for small yachts in England, and they are noted for having little adverse effect on night vision. Beta lights of low magnitude would probably blind the helmsman far less than a binnacle light or illuminated AWI dial. As can be seen in Figure 4-4, one Beta light is attached to the end of a stiff wire rod, which serves as a direction-indication vane that rotates on the shroud, and another Beta light is fixed to the shroud itself. When the two lights draw close together the wind is obviously coming from further ahead, and conversely, when the lights draw apart the wind is more abeam.

A Vanguard sloop. Although this boat is probably not racing, even a cruising helmsman could benefit from luff yarns and telltale windows in the headsail. In this much wind a better practice is to lead the jib sheet through a turning block. For racing to windward in these conditions, the headstay should be tightened to reduce its catenary.

Among the most important visual aids to helmsmanship, especially when beating to windward, are the luff yarns described in the last chapter. These are seen on most boats belonging to serious racers, but yarns are seldom seen on cruising boats, and even a few racing skippers do not use them. In recent years, since luff yarns have come into general use, I think they have been a great equalizer in racing between the mediocre helmsman and the fairly good one, because it is so easy to get a moderately good performance from most boats by simply keeping a few windward and leeward luffs yarns streaming aft (as described in Chapter 3)—provided the sails are properly trimmed, of course. The helmsman simply heads up toward the wind when his leeward yarn begins to twirl around, and he bears off when his windward yarn starts to twirl. The very best steering, however, requires some special interpretation of the yarns and the use of other visual signs and other senses as well. In speaking of interpretation, I mean that an occasional flutter (but not twirling) might be tolerated at the lee side of the luff in the interest of alternately prodding and bearing away from the wind to avoid a choppy wave or responding to a wind fluctuation. Then, too, some boats can be sailed effectively with the windward luff yarns having a definite lift and flutter at times. Quite often it will pay to pinch a boat very slightly in smooth water and moderate wind when she has an ample lateral plane below the water; and some craft with short fin keels might effectively be eased up toward the wind *momentarily* after they have been headed off enough to gain speed and sufficient hydrodynamic lift for puff-prodding.

In order to tell whether the boat is slowing down too much when her windward luff yarns are fluttering, it is desirable to have a good speedometer. The dial should be located as close as possible to the helmsman's normal field of vision, perhaps in the after end of the cabin trunk or above the companionway sliding hatch scabbard. I prefer the type of indicator that has expanded range facilities so that very slight changes in speed can easily be noted. This feature, controlled by a switch, changes the range of the pointer—perhaps increasing a one-knot swing of the pointer to the extent that it appears on the scale as a six-knot swing. For example, if the boat were changing speed by a quarter of a knot—an increment that would be difficult to detect on the unexpanded scale—the expanded reading would show the pointer swinging through 1.5 knots. Obviously, this would not show the *actual* speed change, but what you are interested in is *relative* change, and the expanded scale makes relative change easy to detect.

Aside from the visual aids discussed so far, the helmsman can make use of another clue that I've never seen mentioned in books or magazine articles but that I find quite helpful at times. This is a careful observation of the catenary or sag in the headstay (or jib stay). As mentioned earlier, the headstay should be very taut for the best windward work in moderate to fresh winds, but some sag will always be visible if one looks for it. When the sag is slight, the jib is pulling effectively; but when the stay straightens, the pull of the jib is minimal and its efficiency is being reduced. Of course, you must also consider the gustiness of the wind, and the method doesn't work well in rough seas when the mast is pumping. Nevertheless, sag observation can help in relatively smooth waters and steady winds, and the beauty of this indicator is that the helmsman can watch the stay at the same time he is looking at the luff yarns.

With all these visual aids at the helmsman's disposal, the question of priority naturally arises. On which aid should you concentrate and place the most emphasis? To some extent the answer will depend on the strength of wind and the roughness of the water. In moderate winds when the seas are not rough, the helmsman will usually do best by concentrating on the luff yarn window in his jib and also noting the headstay sag in that area. That field of vision will also permit a peripheral view of the shroud telltale when the helmsman sits to windward. If there is an apparent wind indicator, the helmsman should glance at it occasionally to see whether the boat is near her proper apparent wind angle. Some skippers prefer to have a crew member look at the dial and frequently call out the angle. The next emphasis would normally be placed on the speedometer, and again some skippers like to have a crew member watching the dial and/or judging speed against that of competitors during a race. When the helmsman sitting to windward shifts his eyes away from the sail luffs or his instruments, the purpose should be to look at the water upwind and ahead of the boat This becomes particulary important in heavy weather with rough seas. Under these conditions, in fact, I would give water-watching the number-one priority, because it is most important that the helmsman sail by the seas. He must try to avoid particularly steep waves by luffing above them or bearing off to pass to leeward; and when his boat slows down from pitching or being hit by a wave, he should "give her a rap full" or sail a bit low and concentrate on footing. In very light drifting conditions, water-watching also should take high priority, with the helmsman spending much of his time looking for zephyrs.

Figure 4-5 suggests the order of priority for use of visual

aids when beating in moderate winds. As explained in the legend, numbers in parentheses show the change in emphasis when sailing in heavy winds with choppy seas. Notice that these aids are seen from the windward side of the boat. A lot of helmsmen, even those who are quite skilled, handicap themselves by steering from the leeward side, where they cannot see the waves, the wind on the water, or the luff of the mainsail; and furthermore, they cannot get an advantageous view of the windward shroud telltales when sitting to leeward. Another argument against this steering position on a boat with the normal slight weather helm is that the helmsman must continually push the tiller to steer, but if he sits to windward he merely pulls on the tiller, an action that causes less fatigue and allows a more sensitive feel through the fingers. Needless to say, on a small boat in a fresh wind, the helmsman's weight to weather will help reduce the angle of heel. About the only real argument for steering from the leeward side would be if the helmsman could not see the luff of the jib from the windward side due to a helm location far aft and/or a mast position far forward. In this case, a tiller extension or perhaps a large-diameter wheel will help move the helmsman outboard to improve his visibility from the windward side.

The racing helmsman has two additional important visual aids that should be consulted from time to time—the compass and the inclinometer. Surprisingly, many skippers do not use the compass to detect wind shifts. Severe headers usually necessitate coming about for best progress to windward, but gradual shifts are often hard to detect when no distinctive landmarks are in plain view ahead, unless one keeps track of compass headings. Furthermore, keeping track of these headings will give a better understanding of the pattern of shifts.

The inclinometer is a simple instrument, usually consisting of a curved scale marked in degrees of heeling angle and a pointer in the form of a rigid plumb bob or a bubble or ball in a curved tube filled with liquid. The instrument is important because it shows the exact angle of heel, and every boat has an optimal range of heeling angles that should be learned through trial and error. (More will be said about this subject

FIGURE 4–5: PRIORITY OF VISUAL AIDS

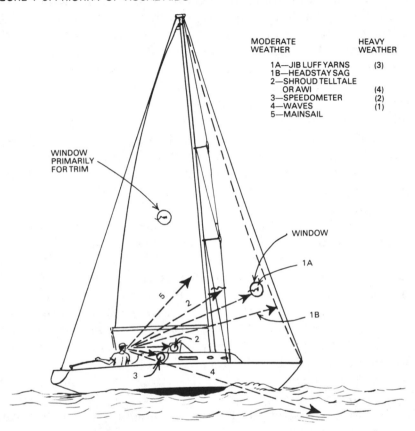

MODERATE WEATHER	HEAVY WEATHER
1A—JIB LUFF YARNS	(3)
1B—HEADSTAY SAG	
2—SHROUD TELLTALE OR AWI	(4)
3—SPEEDOMETER	(2)
4—WAVES	(1)
5—MAINSAIL	

WINDOW PRIMARILY FOR TRIM

WINDOW

1A

1B

in Chapter 5.) During a race it is usually advantageous if the tactician-navigator is assigned to both compass and inclinometer. On elaborate boats repeater dials often are installed over the navigator's desk. The skipper needs only be informed of major or prolonged wind shifts and critical angles of heel— that is, when the boat heels beyond a predetermined angle at which she begins to slow.

All these are visual aids to windward helmsmanship, and sight is the most commonly used and important sense. The best helmsmen, however, use other senses as well. They feel the wind on their faces and hands, sense the change in angle of heel, listen to the sound of water flowing past the hull, listen to the flap of sails, and feel the response of the helm. Of the nonvisual aids I think sail sounds and especially the feel of the helm are the most important. The former is particularly useful at night, because a shaking luff will signal when you are sailing too high. Although some sailmakers encourage the use of cloth tapes to quiet the rattles of sail slides, I prefer stainless steel shackles for securing the slides to the luff, not only because they are stronger but because they make more of a rattle when the luff is shaking. In fact, for night sailing I have thought about using a small bell, like the kind commonly found on cats' collars, taped to the luff of the jib and main (as high up as one can reach) so that shaking luffs are clearly audible.

The feel of the helm comes from water pressure against the rudder, and this pressure varies as the boat changes her angle of heel. When a puff strikes her and she begins to heel, the natural tendency is for her to turn into the wind. Ordinarily, the helmsman should not resist this tendency too much but let the boat turn as she will until the windward luff yarn begins to grow very restless. Then, when the boat starts to right (reduce its heeling angle) there will be less weather helm, and she should usually be headed off a bit. Of course, developing a fine "tiller touch" requires a lot of practice, and different boats often require different techniques. For example, a boat with a long keel and ample lateral plane, as shown in Figure 4-6, might require a gentle touch with a very easy helm action, while the other boat illustrated, having a deep fin that is very short fore and aft, might tolerate a much quicker helm action in the interest of rapid alignment to wind fluctuations. The latter craft probably could not be held as continuously close to the wind at low speeds without the risk of making too much leeway. Of course, these estimates of proper helming depend greatly on other matters such as the displacement of the boat, sea conditions, and the efficiency of the rudders and rigs, but the example illustrates how helm treatment will vary with the characteristics of the boat.

Some sailing manuals show diagrams of velocity made good to windward, commonly abbreviated as Vmg. This is the ac-

FIGURE 4–6: HELM ACTION RELATING TO HULL DESIGN

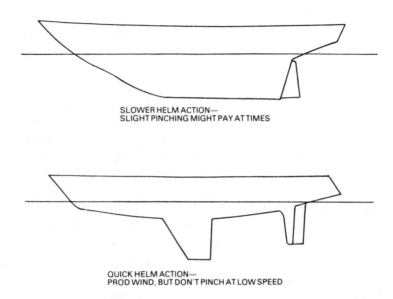

SLOWER HELM ACTION—
SLIGHT PINCHING MIGHT PAY AT TIMES

QUICK HELM ACTION—
PROD WIND, BUT DON'T PINCH AT LOW SPEED

tual progress a boat makes dead to windward as a result of her speed and course relative to the true wind. A typical, smart-sailing racing-cruiser might sail an average course of 28 degrees to the apparent wind for optimim Vmg. If she heads lower (at a greater angle) she will gain speed but not enough to equal her progress to windward on the optimum heading; and if she sails higher than 28 degrees, her heading angle will be more favorable, but speed will drop to make her Vmg less than optimal.

A simple, although somewhat laborious, method to estimate optimum Vmg can be used if the boat is equipped with a speedometer, an anemometer (to tell the velocity of the apparent wind) and an apparent wind indicator to measure the angle of the boat to the apparent wind. The method requires sailing on several headings higher and lower than a full-and-by closehauled course (the one where both windward and leeward luff yarns on a well-trimmed genoa jib are streaming aft). The instruments are read on all headings, and vectors are drawn similar to the ones shown in Figure 4-7. The examples illustrated show the steps necessary to compute the optimal Vmg, which, in this case, is achieved at a heading of 30 degrees. In both vectors the true wind is 8½ knots with apparent winds at about 12 knots. The 40-degree heading produces a boat speed of 6 knots but a Vmg of only slightly over 2; while the 30-degree heading reduces boat speed to 4½ knots but produces Vmg of a little more than 3. Note, however, that leeway is not considered. This is the fly in the ointment, because leeway is so difficult to estimate. It may cause the actual course sailed to be anywhere from 2 to 5 degrees lower than the heading angle. Leeway will vary with the design and type of boat (her keel, rig, and so on), the sea conditions, angle of heel, and especially the heading angle. A boat being pinched may make considerably more leeway than one being sailed full-and-by. Nevertheless, leeway would have to be quite significant to change the conclusion regarding optimum Vmg as illustrated in Figure 4-7, provided the boat were not being pinched too much on the higher heading.

Some sailors make the mistake of doggedly sticking close to the estimated heading for optimum Vmg. This is wrong, because the best heading varies with the wind and seas. In medium winds with smooth seas, a boat might have an optimum Vmg at a heading of 28 degrees, to use a hypothetical case, but in light airs and/or in rough patches of water (powerboat swells, for instance) the same craft might have to be sailed at perhaps 33 degrees. Thus, in typical moderate conditions, when the seas are sometimes smooth and sometimes rough and when the wind is fluctuating in velocity, the proper heading would be a weaving course, varying between optimum headings for the momentary conditions prevailing. Such a weaving course is shown in Figure 4-8, and it should be borne in mind that the headings are irrespective of wind shifts. By way of explanation Figure 4-8 shows light- and medium-wind boat speed curves for all closehauled headings. The further a point on a curve is from point O, the higher the boat speed. The straight lines radiating from point O are the optimum

FIGURE 4-7: SPEED MADE GOOD
              TO WINDWARD (Vmg)

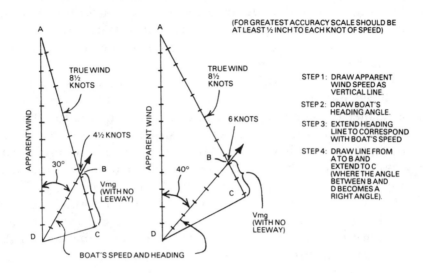

(FOR GREATEST ACCURACY SCALE SHOULD BE
AT LEAST ½ INCH TO EACH KNOT OF SPEED)

STEP 1: DRAW APPARENT
        WIND SPEED AS
        VERTICAL LINE.

STEP 2: DRAW BOAT'S
        HEADING ANGLE.

STEP 3: EXTEND HEADING
        LINE TO CORRESPOND
        WITH BOAT'S SPEED

STEP 4: DRAW LINE FROM
        A TO B AND
        EXTEND TO C
        (WHERE THE ANGLE
        BETWEEN B AND
        D BECOMES A
        RIGHT ANGLE).

FIGURE 4-8: TYPICAL OPTIMUM COURSE
              TO WINDWARD

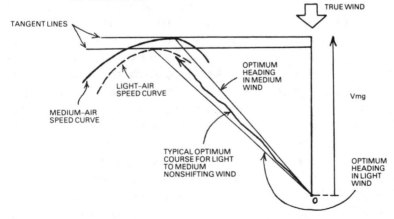

headings for light air with powerboat swells (when sheets are
cracked off a bit) and for moderate wind in smooth water.
Optimum Vmg is found by drawing a perpendicular at right
angles to the true wind direction and just touching the top of

a speed curve (perpendiculars are labeled "Tangent Lines" in Figure 4-8). Obviously, the higher the tangent line the better the Vmg. Notice that in actuality the best course for alternating light to medium wind velocities and varying seas will follow an irregular, weaving line similar to the one shown between the two optimum heading lines.

Proper helmsmanship when coming about varies from boat to boat, and the most effective technique can be determined only after considerable trial-and error experimentation. Nevertheless, some general principles should be kept firmly in mind. A heavy-displacement boat that carries a lot of way should normally be turned more slowly than a light one that stops short when head-to-wind. The former type may gain distance to windward by turning slowly and forereaching, but the latter needs quicker helm action so that she will not have a chance to lose way, at least not before she is headed on the new tack with her sails filled. Of course, any boat with a large, overlapping genoa must be turned rather quickly when she is just past the head-to-wind position so the jib will fill rapidly and blow through the foretriangle area with the leech clear of the spreaders. However, the turning should start slowly and gradually increase in rapidity, as illustrated in Figure 4-9. A rudder jammed hard over initially will stall (especially if it is a spade type), and, of course, it will act as a brake to boat speed. A very common mistake is to turn the boat too far. Seldom if ever should the boat be turned on the new tack much past a course that is at right angles to the original close-hauled course (see Figure 4-9). Although it can be argued that the boat should be allowed to foot off a bit on the new tack before the jib is trimmed in, boat speed has decreased after tacking, and this moves the apparent wind further aft, thus obviating the need to bear away immediately after the tack. Incidentally, it may pay to crack off the main slightly for a moment before the apparent wind draws ahead again, after the boat has regained her speed. The best way to keep from turning the boat too far is to check the compass before tacking to see what the new heading will be or take a rough beam bearing on a landmark. Beginning sailors often make the mistake

FIGURE 4–9: TACKING

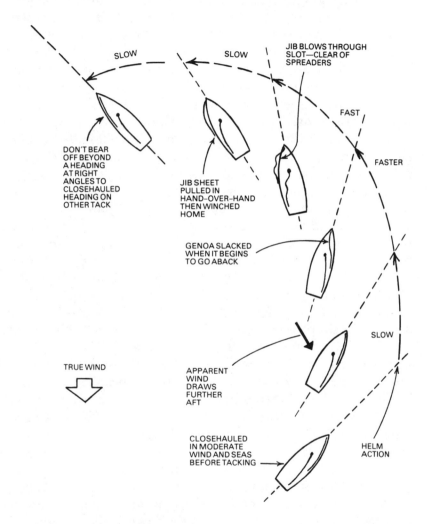

SLOW

SLOW

JIB BLOWS THROUGH
SLOT—CLEAR OF
SPREADERS

FAST

DON'T BEAR
OFF BEYOND
A HEADING
AT RIGHT
ANGLES TO
CLOSEHAULED
HEADING ON
OTHER TACK

JIB SHEET
PULLED IN
HAND–OVER–HAND
THEN WINCHED
HOME

FASTER

GENOA SLACKED
WHEN IT BEGINS
TO GO ABACK

TRUE WIND

APPARENT
WIND
DRAWS
FURTHER
AFT

SLOW

CLOSEHAULED
IN MODERATE
WIND AND SEAS
BEFORE TACKING

HELM
ACTION

of tacking when their boat has insufficient way. This is disastrous to acceleration on the new tack; it causes great leeway before speed is regained; and it may even cause the boat to get in stays in a choppy sea. Needless to say, in a bad seaway the helmsman should try to pick a relatively smooth spot in which to come about.

Downwind

It is generally agreed that beating to windward provides the greatest test of skillful helmsmanship, but steering downwind should never be underrated. On a run especially, incompetent steering will not only lose considerable Vmg to leeward but can even be dangerous in heavy weather. The skilled helmsmen's technique when running is not unlike his method of beating, since it requires a weaving course that varies with wind fluctuations. The principle of bearing off in puffs and heading up in lulls is well known, and it makes all the difference in the speed of a boat downwind; yet many skippers, even racers, do not exploit the technique to full advantage.

Figure 4-10 shows a typical speed curve for Vmg's to leeward at a particular wind velocity. The simplest way to construct one of these curves is to sail the boat downwind in a relatively steady breeze on a variety of headings from a dead run (with the wind directly aft), to a quartering reach (with the true wind 45 degrees from dead aft), and on each heading note the change in boat speed registered on the speedometer. Then plot the headings and speeds as in Figure 4-10. Matters are greatly simplified if you read the boat speed to the nearest tenth of a knot and use a centimeter ruler (with a scale showing tenths) when drawing the headings. If, for example, a certain heading gave a speed of 5.4 knots, the heading line would be drawn 5.4 centimeters long, or, for greater accuracy, you could double the scale and draw the line 10.8 centimeters long. After all the headings sailed have been drawn, you can connect the ends of all the lines with a curved line to give a speed curve. To find the heading producing optimum Vmg to leeward, of course, a tangent line is drawn at right angles to the true wind, but it should be borne in mind that the destination to leeward may not be directly downwind, and thus the best heading is the point on the speed curve where the curve is touched by a tangent line drawn at right angles to the course rhumb line (see dashed tangent in Figure 4-10). In the Figure, the optimum heading for reaching the leeward mark is with the wind 40 degrees form dead aft.

Some sailing manuals recommend constructing the speed

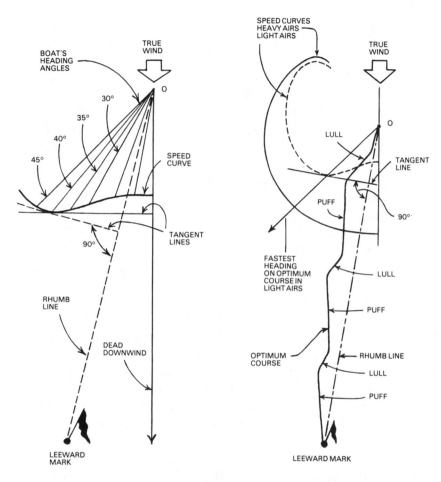

FIGURE 4-10: A DOWNWIND SPEED CURVE

FIGURE 4-11: OPTIMUM COURSE IN VARYING WIND VELOCITIES

curve with headings 5 degrees apart form dead downwind to 30 degrees from dead downwind. In my opinion, however, the headings should be extended to 45 degrees, because in very light airs some boats may optimize their Vmg at this angle by virtue of having a much stronger apparent wind (it should be realized that the further off the wind a boat sails the weaker her apparent wind, because boat speed is subtracted from the true wind velocity). Also, it may not be necessary to plot all headings 5 degrees apart but just those in the vicinity of the estimated optimum Vmg, while the remainder are plotted at 10 degrees.

To make accurate speed curves, of course, it is necessary to have the proper sails set and trimmed to their optimum. When running dead downwind, for example, experiment by bringing the spinnaker pole far aft and heeling the boat to windward to get the spinnaker into completely clear wind. Accuracy also depends on having the precise direction of the true wind. This may be determined by telltales or other wind indicators when on a dead run (on other points of sailing, of course, indicators show only the apparent wind). After the true wind direction has been established on the run, its compass direction is noted, and then each heading is also noted on the compass.

As all experienced sailors know, it usually pays to sail at quite a wide angle (quarter-reaching rather than running) in light airs, but it may pay to head off to nearly a dead run in heavy winds. Thus in winds of varying strength, the optimum course will be a weaving one similar to the optimum course to windward. Figure 4-11 illustrates the situation. The speed curves (often called performance polars) shown in the figure are the curves extended through all points of sailing on the port tack, and the particular ones illustrated are based on the actual performance of a 5.5-meter boat carrying a spinnaker below the beam reach. As explained earlier, the further a point on a curve is from the starting point O, the higher the speed. Notice that the optimum heading in light air is higher than 45 degrees to the true wind considering the location of the leeward turning mark. A mistake some sailors make is not heading high enough on a light-air downwind leg. On the other hand, in a fresh wind, it may pay to sail on a dead run or even slightly by the lee if one can just fetch the mark without jibing.

When the turning mark or destination lies dead to leeward, of course, wide-angle headings in light airs will require tacking downwind—that is to say, reaching off on one tack and then jibing onto the other tack in order to arrive precisely at

the mark. Tacking downwind has less to do with helmsmanship than matters relating to tactics and course strategy such
as playing the wind shifts and tides, therefore this aspect will
be touched on in Chapter 5, which deals with racing.

In heavy winds, the technique of bearing off in puffs is not
only important for optimum Vmg to leeward but also for
safety. Sailing instructors sometimes give the impression to
their students that a boat should always be luffed up into the
wind when she heels too much, but, as mentioned in Chapter
1, a boat sailing off on a broad reach should rarely if ever be
luffed in a strong gust, because she will gain stability more
quickly if she is borne off to a run. As a matter of fact, luffing
up from the broad reach could cause a small centerboard boat
to capsize; such a maneuver adds to the force of the apparent
wind, causes the wind to strike exactly broadside (at which
angle the boat is least stable), and centrifugal force from the
turn is added to (rather than subtracted from) the heeling moment (see Figure 1-3). Many boats, especially those with spade
rudders, which stall easily, will broach to (round up uncon-
trollably into the wind) when they take a knockdown while
broad-reaching; thus it is important for the helmsman to an-
ticipate and react promptly. He should look for approaching
puffs and put the helm up (bear off) with an easy motion at
the first sign of extreme heeling. During the lulls, he can head
higher to average out the course changes.

On headings near the beam reach in moderate winds, many
sailors simply sail a rhumb-line course, but even on this point
of sailing, it often pays during a race to sail a crooked course.
Greatest speeds are usually above the beam reach in light airs,
but below in heavy winds (see Figure 4-11). A weaving course
that goes considerably higher and lower than the beam reach
is seldom possible, however, because it would mean constant
sail changing, alternating between jib and spinnaker. Nevertheless, it may very well pay to carry the spinnaker and head
low on the initial part of the course leg, then set the jib and
sail high on the last part of the leg when the wind is gradually dying; and perhaps vice versa when the wind is freshening.

The author's boat steering herself with a simple vane gear. With the wind forward of the beam and reasonably smooth water, only the slightest movement of the helm is necessary to hold the boat on course. Watching the vane gear in these conditions points out how the usual human helmsman often overreacts when making helm corrections. (Photograph, R. C. Henderson.)

Whether steering a weaving, crooked, or straight course, the helmsman must try not to move his rudder any more than necessary. Excessive rudder movement will slow the boat and make her sail farther than she should. A common fault with novice helmsmen and even more experienced ones is to oversteer, expecially in following or quartering seas. I have often been guilty of this fault, and occasionally I have discovered it by switching to a vane self-steering gear. The vane gear will quite often need to turn the helm only the slightest amount to keep the boat on her course. The vane is not faultless, to be sure, for sometimes in difficult seas it will cause the boat to yaw excessively, but under the right conditions many of us could learn some lessons by watching a self-steering gear. The greatest problem for the human in steering seems to be that he overcorrects to counteract a yaw, and a further difficulty is lack of anticipation. Helm action should begin easily at the first indication that the boat is turning off course. This can often be sensed by changing pressure on the rudder and the beginning of a heel or roll. Of course, the exact technique can never be described; it must be learned through trial and error and practice. But it helps to watch a skilled helmsman or even a good vane gear under the right conditions.

The extent to which one can sail weaving and crooked courses downwind obviously will be limited by sail trim, for the helmsman cannot head up so high that his sails begin to luff, nor should he head off so far that they become stalled or blanketed. There should be a lot of coordination between the sail trimmers and the helmsman. Ideally, the helmsman sticks to optimum headings and the sails are trimmed accordingly, but in actual practice this is not always possible. The sail trimmers cannot react soon enough to rapid wind fluctuations, so the boat must be headed to the angle with the wind at which the sails are correctly trimmed. The spinnaker especially must be properly aligned with the wind very promptly, for it is a sensitive sail and can easily collapse. In light airs it is not always easy for the inexperienced helmsman to tell when a spinnaker is going to collapse and whether the breaking condition is caused by sailing too high or too low. He must pay strict attention to his shroud telltales and masthead wind indicator to tell whether he is luffing or sailing by the lee. A collapse from luffing is usually heralded by the break beginning at the luff and rolling inward toward the center, while a collapse from sailing too low results from the spinnaker's being blanketed and/or stalled, and the 'chute may shakingly fall inward beginning at the leech (the leeward edge of the sail) or middle area. Normally, the helmsman (or sail trimmer) should try to keep the spinnaker "on edge" with its luff just beginning to curl.

The cruising sailor will often run with a "wung-out" jib (with the jib boomed or held by the wind out to windward), since this arrangment gives reasonable speed without the trouble of a spinnaker. Details of the operation will be given in Chapter 6, which deals with cruising seamanship, but it should be said here that sailing with an unboomed wung-out

jib requires close attention to helmsmanship. In order to make
the wind hold the jib out to windward (on the side opposite
the mainsail) without the help of a pole, the helmsman must
sail dead downwind or very slightly by the lee. This means
that the mainsail will be on the verge of jibing, so this sail
must be watched carefully to see that it does not begin to fill
from the forward side. If it begins to bulge inward from forward, then the helmsman must head further up (toward the
wind) to prevent a jibe but not so far that the jib begins to
collapse. Sailing with a wung-out jib requires a very limited
movement of the helm, and in my opinion it should not be
done unless the main boom is vanged or rigged with a preventer, because of the risk of an accidental jibe.

Although veteran cruising sailors are sometimes more profi-
cient in certain areas of seamanship than their racing
brethren, they often lack the sharpness in helmsmanship hewn
by competition. Thus, it is highly recommended that the
enterprising cruising skipper who owns a smartsailing boat
enter an occasional race, if only an informal club race (often
called "mid-week jollies" by the British). This kind of racing,
under a simplified handicap rule, is less serious than formal
competition, but it gives one a chance to practice, test, and
improve his boat handling skills and helmsmanship.

5

Common Errors
Related to Racing

There is a great deal of truth in the old saying that the one who makes the fewest mistakes wins the race. Certainly it is true that when helmsmanship is fairly evenly matched and luck plays no great part, errors in tuning, tactics, and boat handling determine how well one does in a race. Of course, there are many different kinds of mistakes; some are very costly, while others are relatively inconsequential. This chapter will attempt to concentrate on the most common kinds of errors and those most detrimental to one's finishing position.

The Race Committee

Actually, the mistakes that have the potential for causing the greatest amount of harm are those made by the race committee. It is often difficult to find well-qualified committee members, because people who are knowledgeable about racing are usually sailing their own boats or at least crewing for others. Thus it is vitally important that inexperienced committee members be given some basic instructions on running a race, because ignorance of such matters as laying out a course, setting the starting line, designating the proper direction for rounding marks, and setting the finish line can cause collisions or at least complaints and protests.

In laying out a closed course—one that requires a variety of points of sailing and has the finish in the same or nearly the same vicinity as the start—it is highly desirable to have the first leg a beat to windward. The shorter the first leg, the more important it is to have a windward start, because otherwise most of the boats will arrive at the turning mark at about the same time. When a great many boats round a mark simultaneously, protests and collisions can result, or at best some boats are forced into disadvantageous positions that could possibly hurt their chances of finishing well. When many classes are to be started, great care must be taken to assure that the larger boats do not overrun the smaller ones and that the different classes do not reach turning marks at the same time.

On several occasions I have been astonished to learn that some race committee members believe that the perfect windward starting line should be set perpendicular to the rhumb line to the upwind turning mark. This is entirely wrong. Such a starting line should be set *almost* at right angles to the *wind direction* regardless of where the turning mark is located. I say "almost" because it is sometimes desirable that the line be slanted about 5 degrees or perhaps a little less away from a right angle, with the port end of the line moved slightly farther upwind of its squared position (see Figure 5-1). What the race committee should try for is a line that spreads the starting boats as evenly as possible along the line at the starting signal, thus avoiding jams or bunching at either end. Theoretically, every point on the ideal starting line is equally attractive. The reason for slanting the line very slightly away from a perpendicular to the wind on a windward start is that many skippers will prefer to start on the starboard tack at the starboard end of the line, partly because they will be free to tack immediately after starting. A bias of 5 degrees or less as described should make both ends almost equally attractive in average conditions.

Occasionally, it is necessary to have a reaching or running

FIGURE 5-1: WELL-SET LINE FOR A WINDWARD START

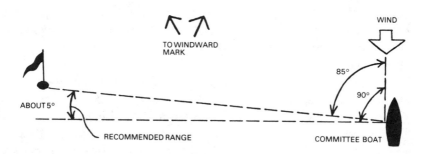

start, and in this case the same principle of not favoring either end of the line also applies. Reaching starts normally require a much greater bias, with the line slanted 15 to 30 degrees away from a perpendicular to the course to the first turning mark. The leeward end should be closer to the turning mark than the windward end. Shifty winds, of course, cause a problem whether the start is to windward or leeward, but the committee should try to set the line with respect to the median of oscillating shifts.

A most important consideration is the length of the starting and finishing lines. When they are too short, collisions are very likely to occur. One simple rule of thumb for the length of a windward starting line is that it should be slightly longer than the product of the number of boats times the overall length of the largest boat. Actually, it is better that the race committee err in having a starting line too long rather than in having one that is too short. Finish lines can and should be much shorter, generally half or less than half the length of the starting line, but occasionally there is real chaos when a lot of boats finish at the same time. On a couple of occasions I have seen boats squeezed off the finish, because there simply was not room for all of them to cross the line simultaneously.

If possible, all turning marks of a closed-course race should be left on the same hand. The port turn is preferable, because boats can approach and turn a mark on the right-of-way starboard tack. A potentially dangerous situation is created if a starboard rounding is designated when the next turning mark lies to the left or vice versa—if a port rounding is designated when the next mark lies to the right. Of course, this means that a boat rounding must make a closed loop, crossing its own track, and there is real danger of collisions. One would not think that race committees could make this mistake, but they have.

Sometimes a source of confusion is the finishing mark. If all the turning marks are left on the same hand, it is generally necessary that either the finishing mark or the committee boat be shifted between the time of the start and the finish. In some cases, however, this is not done, and when there are no specific instructions concerning the finishing mark, confusion can result, especially when the line is not set square to the last leg of the course. I remember when one of the foremost yacht clubs on the East Coast set such a line, and some boats were crossing the line in both directions (first one way and then the other) to be sure of a correct finish. Just after we had crossed, we heard a crash and looked around to witness a collision that resulted in extensive damage, including the loss of a mast.

Some other mistakes I have seen race committees make are: changing signals without calling attention to the changes; allowing the committee boat to drag anchor; not attempting to recall early starters; failing to check that a rounding mark was in place or that its number had not been changed; failing to shorten the course when the wind died out; starting in a calm; not putting an observation boat at the buoy end of the line when it was needed, having a "soldiers" race (all legs reaches); and not putting course instruction placards on both sides of the committee boat when they were needed.

I don't mean to be overly critical of race committees, because running races can involve a lot of responsibility and hard work, and racing sailors should be extremely grateful to those who are willing to serve on the committees. All I am saying is that inexperienced committee members should be given at least rudimentary training and be advised and guided by a few knowledgeable racing sailors. Also, the United States Yacht Racing Union's *Race Committee Manual* should be carefully studied and referred to frequently.

Preparation and Tuning

Most of the time the skipper with a fast boat will be a better tactician than the skipper of a slower boat. I say this because it is so much easier to do the right thing when you have boat speed. You can pull ahead of important competitors and loosely cover them, and if you make a minor mistake you can generally correct it without too great a loss. Furthermore, there is a very definite psychological benefit in having an edge in speed. In contrast, the slower boat must either be subjected to disturbed wind from boats ahead or be forced into the gamble, usually with poor odds, of splitting with the main body of the fleet. There is nothing like a fast boat to make a sailor look good, and that is why it is so important to be meticulous about tuning.

Of course, the aspect of tuning that is probably most beneficial has to do with the set of sails, and this has been discussed in a previous chapter, but of almost equal importance is the condition of the boat's bottom. I'll never forget the frustration I experienced one summer when the bottom of our fiberglass boat developed a severe rash of pinhead blisters. We had had great success racing her the previous year, finishing second in seasonal high-point scoring without really compaigning—that is, by sailing in all the most important events—but one year later the boat seemed unable to get out of her own way. We were sailing poorly, making a lot of mistakes, and consistently finishing near the middle of the class or worse. I can't say how much of our lack of success was due to the actual physical condition of the bottom and how much was due to psychological factors. I did learn that it is important for a skipper to believe that his boat is capable of going fast, and I also know that the bottom was definitely taking the edge off our speed. At any rate, immediately after the bottom was fixed, we went out and sailed three races of an important series, getting two firsts and a third. This was a clear demonstration of the importance of tuning in general and having a good bottom in particular.

Bottom problems with racing boats, especially fiberglass ones, are not at all unusual. Boat builders, gel coat manufacturers, and resin producers do not like to discuss the subject openly, for obvious reasons, but they are aware of the problem and have been researching it for years. Jensen Marine wrote me: "This pin blistering . . . has irritated boat manufacturers for a decade and no one is any closer to a solution now than they were ten years ago." Underwater blisters can occur in the bottom paint, gel coat, or laminate, and they can form for a variety of reasons. Some of these are: poor quality or adulterated resin; improper spraying of gel coat or chopped glass and resin; failure to roll out air bubbles in laminate layers; improper resin saturation of the layers; poor materials (often auto-body compounds) used for fairing and patching (especially around keels); improper thickness of gel coat; failure to remove the mold releasing agent completely before painting; failure to roughen the gel coat surface before painting; and so forth. New boats often have a problem with curing. According to one theory, plasticizer or styrene may migrate and combine with water penetrating the bottom paint or gel coat, causing a hydrolysis that forms the blisters. When the gel coat is thin, paint blisters may result; but when it is thick, blisters may form in the gel coat itself.

The best way to repair a blister condition is probably to cut out the large laminate blisters, let them dry thoroughly, and fill them with an epoxy mastic or polyester putty. With an extensive rash of smaller blisters, it may be best to remove the bottom paint, sand the gel coat thoroughly, removing the blisters, and cover the bottom with at least two coats of clear epoxy resin. This will form a good barrier between the chemicals and the water. Then, of course, a good antifouling paint is applied over the epoxy. This is an expensive treatment, but it is effective and long-lasting, at least in our case and several others with which I am familiar.

As for the bottom paint, by all means use one that is highly antifouling in salt water areas when haulouts are limited. I don't think there is any real substitute for high copper content to discourage barnacles and speed-retarding marine growth. We used one of the most copper-rich paints for a recent Atlantic voyage lasting over two months, and the bottom stayed clean as a whistle, although there were prominent gooseneck barnacles all over the boot top and counter above the water-line where there was no antifoulant. The most effective, rela-tively soft copper paints are rough when they are first applied, but they can be smoothed up with *very light* rubbing, using fine wet-and-dry paper or bronze wool.

Old-timers used to say that slime made a boat fast, but this notion was later scoffed at by racing sailors. Some fairly recent research, however, has revealed that a very slight amount of certain long-chain polymer algae—just enough to make the bottom feel slippery—can indeed beneficially affect the behav-ior of the water flow next to hull, known as the boundary layer. The algae tend to damp the molecular oscillations within the boundary layer and extend laminar flow (the smooth attached flow at the forward part of the keel and hull). Many sailors engage divers to clean and wet-sand their boat bottoms just before an important race, but it is often better to do this a few days before the race. Furthermore, one should be extremely cautious about oversanding the bottom, as this can remove the paint and destroy the effectiveness of the antifoulant. It is also usually better to wait several days or a week before racing after the bottom has been freshly painted with soft antifoulant.

Fairing the bottom is no less important than smoothing it. Through-hull fittings should be made flush with the bottom; ridges, bumps, dents, and sharp corners should be leveled or filled with a fairing compound such as epoxy putty or epoxy resin mixed with phenolitic microballoons; flexible fairing pieces might be added to improve the gap between the rudder and the after edge of the keel or skeg; underwater transducers and sensors for instruments should be as inconspicuous as possible; and of course all underwater appendages should be streamlined and have provisions for deflecting seaweed with either slanted leading edges or separate weed deflectors. It is not always realized that the boundary layer is much thinner forward than aft, and so special attention should be given to the bow and leading edges of the keel, skeg, and forward part of a spade rudder. A frequently neglected part of the bottom, incidentally, is the underside of the keel.

Of course, the propeller is a major source of underwater drag. When a solid (nonfolding and nonfeathering) prop is used, be sure it is of a size and pitch that minimizes drag without too much sacrifice of performance under power. Prominent rating rules usually limit the pitch angle between the shaft line and the face of the blade to 45 degrees in order for the prop to obtain the rating advantages of being solid. Also there is often a minimum performance requirement that the power installation must be capable of propelling the boat at a certain speed—for example, a speed in knots of 0.75 times the square root of the rated length. Needless to say, the pertinent rules should be studied so that one can take maximum legal advantages of propeller allowances.

Of course, feathering and especially folding props will be costly in rating because of their low drag, but they are usually worth the penalty when the propeller is exposed—that is, when it is not close behind a keel or skeg. Care must be taken to see that a folding prop has its shaft marked to indicate when the pin on which the blades hinge is vertical so that the lower blade will not fall open. Occasionally a mistake is made in marking the shaft when the blade line (the line made by the tips of the blades when they are folded together) rather than the pin is vertical. This is explained in Figure 5-2. Actually it is possible for a blade to fall open even when the pin is vertical on an upright boat if she takes a knockdown, and that is why I prefer blades fitted with magnets such as those made by the Michigan Wheel Corporation. Folding and feathering props must be kept well lubricated, and usually they should not be painted because of the risk that the paint might cause the blades to bind when opening or closing. A coating that has been used on propellers with apparent success is a product called Sea-Film made by the Columbian Bronze Corporation. It is a slippery, electrolysis-inhibiting coating that also seems

FIGURE 5-2: FOLDING PROP AND ITS ALIGNMENT

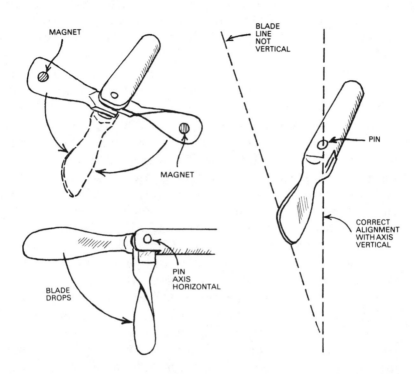

to discourage barnacles. Incidentally, the cotter pins on folding props should be hammered flat, as they can snag seaweed.

Tuning a boat also includes such factors as weight distribu-
tion, hull trim, and finding the optimal angle of heel. It is
generally agreed that weight should be concentrated amidships
to minimize pitching in a seaway. This means that tanks, ballast, and other major weights should be located as near as
possible to the longitudinal center of gravity, and heavy gear
should be kept out of the ends. It is not always realized, however, that there may be times when moving crew weight in the
longitudinal direction away from the center can be advantageous. For instance, steering might be more easily controlled on
a heavy-weather run if the crew moves aft, and in light air,

wetted surface might be reduced slightly if the crew moves forward. Also, on a heavy-weather reach when maximum beam is fairly far aft, stability might be improved by keeping the crew on the windward rail abaft amidships. Every effort should be made to minimize weight at the masthead, because weight aloft not only is harmful to stability but increases the tendency to pitch because of its great distance from the boat's center of rotation.

As mentioned in the last chapter, every boat has an optimal heeling angle range. For instance, she might sail her fastest between the angles of 10 and 20 degrees of heel. The optimal range will vary for different boats and different conditions, and it can only really be found through experimentation with close attention to the speedometer. As a general rule, boats with flat bilges and broad beam amidships do not like to be heeled very much, while narrower boats with slack bilges and long overhangs pick up speed with a moderate heel. Almost any boat, of course, will lose speed when her rail becomes submerged; yet it is surprising to see how often boats are sailed with their decks awash. In these conditions, a reef will reduce the heeling angle and reduce excessive weather helm, increase projected sail area, increase keel efficiency, reduce drag, and thus improve speed. In light airs, however, many boats will sail faster with a slight angle of heel, because their sails will hang in a better shape, waterline length will be increased, helm balance may be improved, and in some cases wetted surface may be decreased somewhat.

Hull trim should be considered not only from the standpoint of what produces the best speed and resistance to heel when under sail but also from the standpoint of how it will affect the handicap rating of the boat. In most cases, of course, a boat will perform well and look her best when she floats on her designed load waterline, but under most handicap rules she will very often have the best rating without undue sacrifice to speed with a slight bow-down trim. One reason is that waterline length will usually be shortened. In addition, most racing-cruisers will lose some initial stability (because their maximum waterline beam is abaft amidships), which will tend to help their

A "soldier's" leg, with the close-reaching boats that are not in the lead being forced to sail in the wakes and dirty air of the leaders. These yawls can be sailed effectively at moderate angles of heel, because their long overhangs increase the waterline length when the boats heel. (Official U. S. Navy photograph, courtesy of the U. S. Naval Institute.)

rating under rules such as the IOR and CCA that measure and penalize stability (see Figure 5-3 for an explanation). Still another reason that a bow-down trim may be desirable under the IOR is that it can be helpful to the immersed depth measurements. Of course, the rating rule or measurer nearly always puts a limit on how much the boat can be trimmed, but it usually pays to take full advantage of that limit. Another consideration is that small boats often need to be trimmed down by the bow somewhat to offset crew weight in the cockpit. A lot of heavy gear and stores may be helpful to rating, especially when the weight is kept forward, but it may be harmful to speed. A very common mistake is to have the boat measured when it is light and then permit the accumulation of heavy supplies. The racing skipper should make every attempt to keep the boat as light as she was when measured.

FIGURE 5-3: CHANGING THE RATING BY ALTERING
TRIM

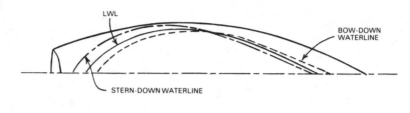

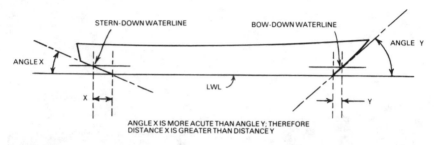

ANGLE X IS MORE ACUTE THAN ANGLE Y; THEREFORE
DISTANCE X IS GREATER THAN DISTANCE Y

Aside from trimming and loading the boat advantageously, there are other frequently neglected ways to optimize the handicap rating. Most boats have their spars banded (marked with black bands that limit sail size) to obtain optimum sail area rating. In many cases, however, the sails are much smaller than the distances between the bands. This can be corrected by moving the bands to the point where they just touch each corner of the sail when its luff and foot are under medium tension. When further tensioning is needed, Cunningham cringles and flattening reef cringles can be used as described in Chapter 3. Also, a light-air stretchy-luff jib can be made full size when it has a Cunningham cringle just above the tack. Incidentally, the spinnaker foreguy can be made to double as a Cunningham downhaul for the jib when it is led through a block at the tack.

Many racing skippers do not take full advantage of the customary practice of rounding off decimals in the final calculation of a rating. Most calculations are carried out to four decimal places, but the actual assigned rating is resolved to the nearest tenth of a foot; thus .05 of a foot will resolve to .1

but .049 will be .0. The entire range from .95 through 1.049 will be rounded off to 1 foot of rating, yet there is almost a tenth of a foot between the extremes of the range. This means that the racing skipper may be able to change the location of his black bands very slightly to lower the rating a tenth of a foot or else add a slight amount of sail area without raising his rating. Most sailmakers are equipped with computers and can help optimize rated sail area for a small fee whether or not sails are ordered.

The skipper should check to see that there are no unnecessary penalties on battens that are too long or oversize sails such as drifters or other specialized sails that are used relatively infrequently. Also, very careful consideration should be given to oversize spinnaker poles that carry a rating penalty. Unless the foretriangle is unusually tall and narrow, I think it normally pays to keep the spinnaker pole the exact length of the *J* measurement (the base of the foretriangle). At least, it seems safe to say that the pole should not be any shorter than *J*, because one normally wants the longest possible pole without paying a penalty for it. Your sailmaker can be helpful with these decisions.

An important part of preparation for racing is crew instruction. Sail handling mistakes can be extremely costly; thus every effort should be made to train inexperienced crew members and see that they are familiar with all the gear on your boat. As mentioned in Chapter 1, it is a good idea to label sheet leads and all parts of the running rigging. Use consistent sail-handling procedures and stowage plans, and get in the habit of double-checking such procedures as laying out the spinnaker gear, bending sails, and rigging extra sheets or any special racing gear.

Also, of course, the skipper and/or navigator-tactician must be well prepared in matters relating to weather, tides, navigation, racing rules, and race instructions. They should listen to weather forecasts and look at the latest synoptic charts, read the tidal current tables and charts, review the United States Yacht Racing Union rules, study the racing instructions carefully, and plot courses with headings noted on local navigation charts. Attention to these matters will be helpful not only in the practical sense but in the psychological sense as well. It is important for the skipper and crew to know in their own minds that they are well prepared for the race.

The Start

It has often been said that races are won or lost at the start. For the most part, this applies only to one-design or level racing boats (those with the same handicap rating) sailing short courses. However, a bad start can be a serious disadvantage for any boat, even one sailing a race of considerable length, because a late starter might be forced to sail for some time in turbulent air created by the fleet ahead of him, or he might be forced to take a disadvantageous tack in order to clear his air.

Most experts seem to agree that the primary considerations in getting a good start are making sure you will have the ability to go where you want and making sure you can obtain clear air immediately after the start. Some sailors, including me, make the mistake of nearly always starting at the "favored end" of the line, even when doing so prevents them from going where they want right after the starting signal. One end is favored, of course, when the line is not squared to the wind and a boat luffing head-to-wind at the middle of the line is pointed closer to one end than the other. The end toward which the bow is headed is the one favored, because a boat starting there will be ahead of a boat starting at the opposite end (see Figure 5-4). A start at the favored end is often advantageous, especially if there is a lot of bias to the line, but again, it is a mistake to start there when you will be forced to sail on the wrong tack or in disturbed air.

As an example, I remember starting a race on the starboard tack at the favored port end when the port tack was the correct one to be on, due to the effects of a strong current. Our start was a good one, but we were unable to tack and clear the starboard tack boats behind and to windward. By the time we were able to tack, it was too late. We were out in the adverse current, and the boats that had started at the starboard end of the line and had been able to tack immediately were far ahead.

Another example of a time when one might not start at the favored end would be if the starboard end were strongly favored and boats were barging and jamming at the mark (or committee boat). In that case, it might be better to start a bit farther down the line in clean air. If you can hit the line at top speed as the gun goes off, you will have a good lee bow position with clear wind while many of your competitors to windward are sailing in disturbed air.

Quite often skippers will determine which end of the line is favored a long time before the start, but a certain number of these sailors will fail to keep a check on wind shifts. Obviously, a significant shift could completely change the situation and cause the opposite end to be favored (see Figure 5-4). It is usually a good idea to keep track of the wind direction with the compass and to luff the boat up head-to-wind frequently in order to check on shifts. Also, a crew member should be assigned the task of watching the wind direction as shown by flags on the committee boat and the courses of close-hauled boats, especially boats in classes starting before you. In an oscillating wind it is important to time the shifts so that you can improve your chances of predicting the favored end at the time of the start and to be in phase with the shifts during the beginning of the first windward leg.

One of the most common mistakes made at the start is getting too far away from the line. This error is particularly fre-

FIGURE 5-4: CHOOSING THE FAVORED END OF THE STARTING LINE

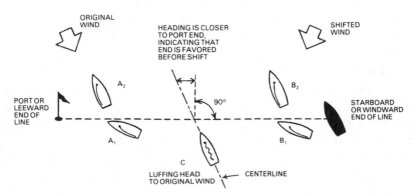

quent when big boats are starting in light air. It is more difficult to keep a big boat close to the line because of its relatively
sluggish maneuverability and less easily manageable headsails;
thus a frequent starting technique is to use a timed start—
making a reach away from the line and then back toward it so
that the boat hits the line at the starting signal. In light airs,
however, the boat should make only a very short reach away
from the line; otherwise she might hit a calm spot that could
make her very late.

Another reason why boats are sometimes late for the start is
that their jibs are not hoisted soon enough, and very often the
sail is set while headed away from the line. If there is any
foul-up while hoisting, the boat is often late. It is a great
temptation to delay setting a large genoa jib, because it blocks
visibility and creates some handling difficulties, but I, for one,
have learned my lesson that the sail should be set at least ten
minutes before the start. Late starts can also occur because the
crew is practicing tacking and trying out different sails or
shortening down just before the start. All of these things must
be done well in advance, because it is often surprising how far
you can get away from the line when you are concentrating
on sails, crew work, or other matters not directly concerned
with the start.

The matter of a genoa jib blocking visibility is a serious
one, because the modern deck-sweeping type compeletly
blocks the view ahead to leeward when it is trimmed in flat.
The only answer is to have an experienced crew member stationed in the pulpit forward of the jib prior to the start. He
must signal the helmsman when a boat is approaching or being approached in the blind sector. Of course, it is most important for the helmsman to watch the bow man as well as
keep a lookout in the sectors of good visibility. It will be helpful if the jib sheet can be kept well eased until just before the
start, because this permits the clew to go forward and the foot
to lift, which will greatly improve visibility. One tip given to
me by Philip Marriner, manager of Hard Sails, is to rig a
piece of shock cord from a grommet in the foot to one of the
lower jib hanks as illustrated in Figure 5-5 in order to lift up

The designer, Halsey Herreshoff, at the helm of a Bristol 33. The forward helm position has certain drawbacks, such as reduction of visibility, but one seldom-considered advantage on a racing boat is that the position restricts a competitor's luffing rights under USYRU rule no. 38.1. (Photograph courtesy of John Sherwood III.)

The author as a horrible example. Finishing a race back in 1960, the author's boat is shown with her main trimmed too far to leeward so that it is badly backwinded. This fault might be relieved not only by centering the main boom, but also by cracking the jib sheet. The boat's fore-and-aft trim and her motion in the conditions shown are not being helped by the man sitting on the bow. At the start this would be a good place for a lookout, but after that he should normally be stationed much further aft on a boat of this size or smaller. (Photograph, Fred Thomas.)

FIGURE 5-5: LIFTING THE FOOT OF A GENOA BEFORE THE START

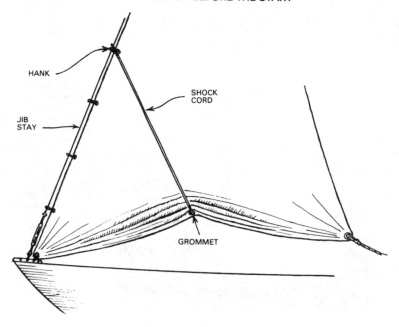

the skirt and allow a view under the foot. Obviously, this will not help the shape of the jib, but it will do no harm when jockeying for position before the start, and the shock cord can be released just before the gun when the jib is trimmed in for optimum pointing.

A good method of staying close to the line without killing too much way or getting a lot of disturbed air is to utilize the port-tack approach from the port side of the line. Many sailors are reluctant to use this method for fear of fouling starboard tackers, and it is true that under rule 34b a starboard tacker may "assume a proper course to start." However, a starboard tacker may not deliberately balk or alter course (except to assume the proper starting course) in an attempt to prevent the port tacker from keeping clear. Normally, the boat using the port-tack approach comes about onto starboard tack just before the starting signal. The usual technique is to approach from port and tack just ahead of the first starboard tackers (but don't tack too close), and if the fleet is late for the line your start should be almost perfect. If the fleet is a bit early, however, you tack, then slack sheets, luff, and let the first boats that approach from starboard pass to leeward of you (they will seldom pass to windward for fear of being luffed over the line). By the time they get clear of you, through your wind shadow, they should be far enough to leeward so as not to disturb your air provided you do not have to kill too much way and can trim sheets for reasonable speed and pointing ability just before the gun. If the skipper who approaches on the port tack finds that the first starboard tackers are quite early, he should pass through the first group of boats and tack into the first gap he finds. Of course, when the starboard tackers are very early, the boat approaching on port should pass through or under the entire starboard fleet and come about astern of it.

Many a promising starting plan has been disrupted by failure to consider the current. A strong fair current may put you over the line too early, while a foul current can make you late. Then, too, there is a wonderful opportunity to capitalize on the mistakes of others. For example, a dip start (dipping down from the windward side of the line) is often successful when the main body of the fleet is late due to a foul current; while a fair current gives the opportunity for a late start at the starboard end of the line when that end is favored, because early starters will tend to run down the line toward the leeward end to kill time, often leaving a beautiful gap through which you can start (see Figure 5-6). Despite the importance of current, it is surprising to see the number of sailors who don't check it. Always sail to the buoy end of the line prior to the start to see how fast and in what direction the current is flowing. Don't merely rely on what the tables predict, for they are often inaccurate.

A serious mistake that is still made today, although not as often as it was some years ago, is to demand buoy room at the starboard end of the starting line. In former times this was legal, but not so today, not even after the starting gun (before crossing the line), for the leeward boat can squeeze out the one

FIGURE 5-6: CURRENT AT THE STARTING LINE

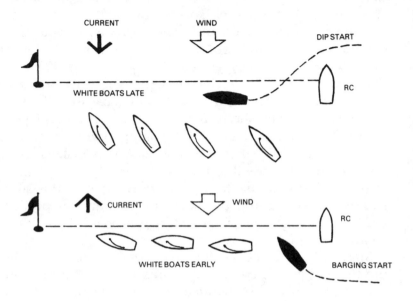

FIGURE 5-7: SPLITTING TACKS WITH A COVERING BOAT

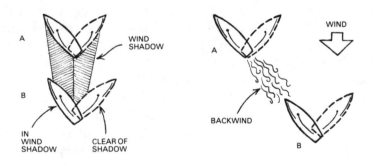

to windward so long as she is not headed above the course to
the first mark or above closehauled. The importance of being
familiar with the latest racing rules would seem obvious, but
many racing skippers are deficient in this respect. Even during
a multimillion-dollar challenge for the America's Cup, in

which no effort was spared in any department, the Australians in 1970 were disqualified from one race because of a misunderstanding regarding the so-called antibarging rule (no. 42.3).

Strategy and Tactics

One of the greatest mistakes in regard to boat-for-boat tactics, in my opinion, is to tight-cover a competitor while fleet racing. By tight-covering I mean for the leading boat to stay close to a competitor in such a way that the competitor is given bad air in the form of wind shadow or backwind. In the first place, I have always felt that a tightly covered boat may well be able to break that cover on a beat when the boat speeds are equal (or the covered boat is faster). The covered boat has the advantage of being able to initiate the action and thus come about slightly quicker (boat speed and crew work being equal) when it is desirable to split tacks to clear her wind, and on one tack (either port or starboard) her wind will be relatively undisturbed. This is illustrated in Figure 5-7. Notice that in each case when the boats are on the starboard tack, *B* has her wind disturbed, but when both boats are on the port tack, *B* has clear wind. If *A* is even slightly faster than *B*, of course, the latter can seldom if ever break cover, but then there is no reason to cover, except perhaps in a special case when there is a need to beat a particular rival to win a series. In this case, however, it is nearly always better to use a loose cover, meaning that you merely try to stay approximately between your rival and the next mark. The main drawback with any covering tactic is that preoccupation with any one competitor will be disadvantageous with respect to the rest of the fleet. Try to avoid getting involved in costly tacking duels and luffing matches. Except under very special circumstances, it nearly always pays to sail your own race.

The most important aspect of strategy has to do with the current and wind, of course, The current is relatively easy to observe and predict, but the wind is much more difficult, at least when it comes to prognostication. Obviously, weather forecasts are very helpful, especially those that predict wind strength, direction, and major shifts; but such forecasts are based on the movement and development of the general weather system, and they are often inaccurate when applied to a short race in a particular local area. Many times a wind shift will occur as forecast but will do so hours after the race is over. The actual behavior of the wind in the racing area is influenced by local factors such as geographical and topographical features of the land and body of water. Land-sea breezes caused by unequal heating of the land and water play an important part.

There is no way that even a trained meteorologist can consistently make chronologically accurate predictions of wind change within a particular limited area based on knowledge of the general weather system alone. To make reasonably accurate forecasts within an average closed-course day race, one must have plenty of local knowledge. This is best obtained by experience and keeping a record of observations over a period of time. It is surprising how often wind changes repeat themselves and follow similar patterns under a given set of conditions. A great many racing sailors make a mistake in not keeping accurate records of the weather conditions during their races.

Most yacht clubs have preplanned courses that make extensive use of fixed government buoys so that the same set of courses is used year after year. One standard course usually is used for each prevailing wind direction. After each race the skipper should record the course, the wind strength and direction at the time of the start, the general weather condition, the state of the current, the approximate temperature of the land and water, wave conditions, wind shifts or changes in strength during the race, mistakes made by him and his crew, and a brief analysis of the correct strategy (for instance, why the leaders profited by tacking toward the windward rather than the leeward shore). Many successful veteran skippers carry this kind of information in their minds, but exact details, such as the nature of the general weather system, are difficult to remember. It is far better, for less experienced sailors at least, to keep a sort of shorthand notebook of observations and conclusions. Of course, this will by no means guarantee success, but it will improve one's chances of doing well and lead to gradual improvement. Furthermore, it will add another dimension of interest to racing.

There is not much point in knowing how the wind will shift unless you can place your boat in the right location to take advantage of the shift. Most racing sailors know the basic rules for beating in shifty winds: take the close tack to the mark, tack on headers, and don't sail out to the lay line. However, many skippers (myself included) do not take full advantage of the rules, nor do they always fully understand the exceptions.

It is common practice for dinghy sailors to tack almost every time there is a significant heading shift, and tremendous gains are possible when this is done correctly; but many big-boat sailors are reluctant to use the technique for fear of losing too much ground when coming about. Part of the answer is for the big-boat sailors to improve tacking technique so that they too can take some advantage of possible upwind gains. Of course, practice will help speed up tacks. It is important that the jib sheet not be slacked until head-to-wind, and after falling off on the new tack, a crew member or two should pull aft on the clew to minimize winch cranking. A seldom-used wrinkle to improve acceleration is to crack off the mainsheet until full speed is regained.

Of course, the big boat should not be tacked as often as a dinghy, and obviously the nature of the shift must be considered. For instance, it will not pay to tack on rapidly oscillating shifts. Nevertheless, many big boats are not tacked often enough. I vividly remember crewing on a medium-displacement cruising sloop when the racing fleet divided on a beat, half the fleet going to one shore and half going to the opposite shore. Despite a moderate foul current, we stayed in the middle, tacking on every shift that headed us by more than approximately 10 degrees, and we reached the windward mark far ahead of the other boats in our class and indeed ahead of many larger boats in the class that started ten minutes before us.

An important exception to the "tack on headers" rule is that boats should not be tacked excessively in light airs, especially boats that are slow in stays. In very light airs the main consideration should be to stay in the patches of wind and keep the boat moving. Seldom should you tack except to reach a new wind. It is a very common error to come about too often in calm weather. Incidentally, it is often a mistake to think that light-displacement boats can be tacked more frequently than heavy boats, because, although the former will accelerate more rapidly, they lose way more quickly and normally have less sail area and shorter masts, which do not reach up into the fresher winds aloft.

As said before, you should not tack in an attempt to take advantage of rapidly oscillating shifts. About the only way you can tell how long such temporary shifts will last is to time them and try to get a feeling for their pattern. It is often helpful if a crew member, perhaps the tactician, can watch the telltales and course changes and glance at his timepiece or even mentally count off the seconds between wind fluctuations, thus leaving the skipper or helmsman free to concentrate on sailing the boat.

Another exception to the rule regarding immediate tacking in headers has to do with those shifts often known as wind bends. These are relatively permanent shifts in a given wind that are caused by the geography or topography of the land. Figure 5-8 shows four typical examples of wind bends: past an island, around a point, down a river, and along a shore. The areas between the dashed lines and shore indicate regions of calm or disturbed wind, while the areas between the dotted lines and shore show approximate regions of increased wind. Long solid arrows, of course, show the directional flow of wind. The boats illustrated are for the most part following advantageous courses, because they are avoiding the calm or disturbed regions, taking advantage of the wind bends (notice that they are lifted more than they are headed), taking advantage of the regions of increased wind, and whenever possible sailing into waters where the seas should be relatively smooth.

Wind bending is not entirely predictable because of such factors as irregular altitude of the land, gaps in the shoreline through which the wind can funnel, thermal conditions, and so forth. Still, it is clear that an entirely different strategy should be used for wind bends than is used with general persistent or oscillating shifts. With the latter it nearly always pays to tack at once on a major header, but with the former it pays to sail well into the header, normally standing in toward the shore as far as possible short of reaching the blanketed area before tacking. The novice racer should make every effort to learn to distinguish between shifts and wind bends by studying the charts, observing the effects of the wind on himself and competitors, and discussing the subject with experienced local sailors.

As can be seen in Figure 5-8, it sometimes pays to tack toward a wind bend lift on a beat, but it seldom pays to tack toward an expected lift in a general wind shift, and this is a frequent mistake made by inexperienced racers. This trap is understandable, because one would normally think it is helpful to be lifted, but you must think how the shift is going to affect you on the other tack. The situation is explained in a simple way in Figure 5-9. Boat *A*, taking the tack toward the expected header, comes about immediately after being headed and can fetch the windward mark, whereas boat *B*, sailing toward the expected lift, has the longer distance to sail. The reason that this rule is not necessarily true with wind bends is that those shifts are usually quite localized, and a boat sailing into such a lift is often lifted for a longer perion of time than she is headed after tacking (see Figure 5-8). Then too, there are the other factors already mentioned, such as smoother water and increased wind velocity, aside from current strategy (not yet discussed), which often encourages hugging shore when the flow is adverse.

In his classic book *Race Your Boat Right*, Arthur Knapp lays down the law in no uncertain terms when he says, "Always take the tack which is closest to your mark." This refers to the case where the upwind mark is not dead to windward and you can point closer to it on one tack than on the other. The reasoning behind this rule is that a lifting shift on the close tack may allow the boat to fetch the mark, while a severe header will allow her to come about and nearly fetch on the

FIGURE 5-8: WIND BENDS

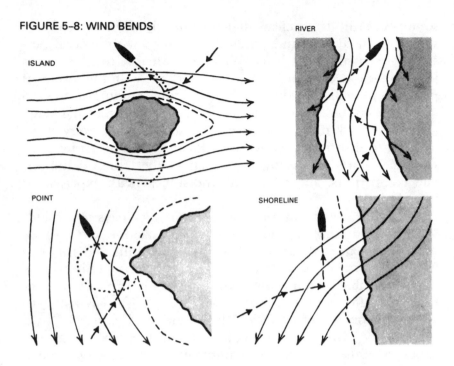

FIGURE 5-9: BEATING TOWARD
A WIND SHIFT

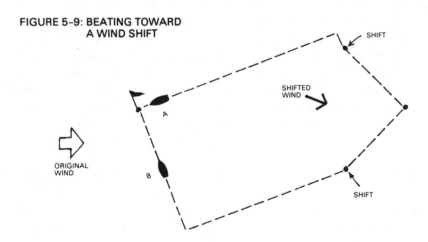

FIGURE 5–10: EXCEPTION TO CLOSE-TACK RULE

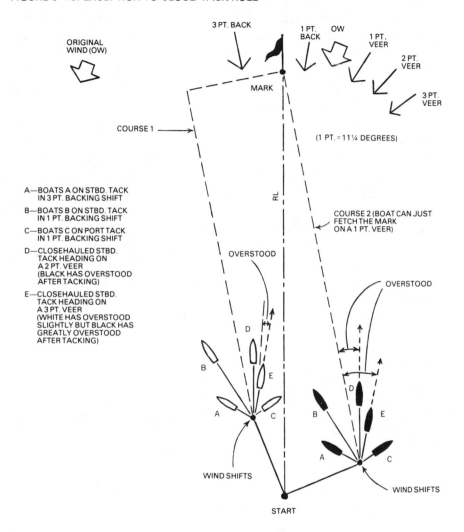

ORIGINAL WIND (OW)

3 PT. BACK

1 PT. BACK

OW

1 PT. VEER

2 PT. VEER

3 PT. VEER

MARK

COURSE 1

(1 PT. = 11¼ DEGREES)

A—BOATS A ON STBD. TACK IN 3 PT. BACKING SHIFT

B—BOATS B ON STBD. TACK IN 1 PT. BACKING SHIFT

C—BOATS C ON PORT TACK IN 1 PT. BACKING SHIFT

D—CLOSEHAULED STBD. TACK HEADING ON A 2 PT. VEER (BLACK HAS OVERSTOOD AFTER TACKING)

E—CLOSEHAULED STBD. TACK HEADING ON A 3 PT. VEER (WHITE HAS OVERSTOOD SLIGHTLY BUT BLACK HAS GREATLY OVERSTOOD AFTER TACKING)

COURSE 2 (BOAT CAN JUST FETCH THE MARK ON A 1 PT. VEER)

RL

OVERSTOOD

OVERSTOOD

D

E

B

A

C

D

E

B

A

C

WIND SHIFTS

WIND SHIFTS

START

COURSE 1 IS LONGER THAN COURSE 2 (EXCEPTION TO THE CLOSE-TACK RULE)

WHITE BOATS ARE AHEAD OF BLACK BOATS

opposite tack. The rule is certainly well recognized, but I don't think one can be entirely dogmatic about its use. There is an important exception that occurs when the close tack takes you toward a slight lift that does not allow you to fetch. In this case, the boat taking the far tack first runs into a slight header that allows him to tack and fetch. This is explained in Figure 5-10. Notice that the positions of boats are shown during a variety of early veers (clockwise wind shifts) and backs (counterclockwise shifts). The white boats are ahead of the black ones, but a black boat will beat the white one to the mark on a 1-point veer (see courses 1 and 2 in the diagram).

To generalize, it would seem that the best policy is to temper use of the rule with such factors as the extent, time, and direction of expected wind shifts and also how far away the upwind mark is from being dead to windward. For instance, if the mark is not far from being dead to weather, it will probably pay to tack toward an expected header. Even when the mark can almost be fetched on one tack, it may pay to take a very short hitch on the far tack in the interest of clearing one's wind with respect to boats ahead. Then too, in special cases the far tack may get one into better wind or current.

The rule advising not sailing out to the lay line is a good one, because once you are on that line where you can just fetch the windward mark, any wind shift will theoretically hurt you. Perhaps the most valuable aspect of the rule is that it prevents sailors from overstanding the mark, a surprisingly frequent mistake. However, the rule should not be followed blindly, for at some times it may very well pay to sail out to the lay line. One such case might be during a light-air race when it is usually advantageous to stick to one side of the course for better wind or tide and also to avoid the excess tacking required when sailing up the middle of the course. Furthermore, with large boats, especially, in light airs, it is often advisable to sail slightly past the lay line and overstand just a bit when quite close to the mark, because it is not worth the gamble of having to make two extra tacks if you are headed and cannot fetch. When on the lay line or slightly higher

A revealing aerial view of a yacht race. Notice the wakes at the turning mark, which show how the boats that turn wide initially have the weather berth over the boats that cut close to the mark initially and then turn.

close to the mark, a wind shift will not seriously hurt you, because a header may very well allow you to fetch by pinching, and a lift will allow you to crack sheets and pick up some extra speed.

There is often a problem in crowded fleets of having a parade of starboard-tack boats approach the windward mark on the lay line. Ordinarily, one tries to approach the mark on the right-of-way tack, but when there is a parade (one boat closely behind another) the wind near the lay line is badly disturbed. If the mark is to be left to starboard, one solution to the problem of getting clean air is to make a port-tack approach. This is not overly risky with the mark left to starboard, because the port-tack boat has the advantage of not having to tack at the mark, and if she stays above the lay line she can luff clear of a

FIGURE 5–11: WINDWARD MARK LEFT TO STARBOARD

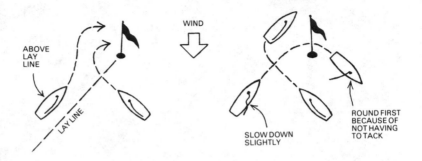

WIND

ABOVE
LAY
LINE

LAY LINE

SLOW DOWN
SLIGHTLY

ROUND FIRST
BECAUSE OF
NOT HAVING
TO TACK

starboard tacker rounding as illustrated in Figure 5-11. Quite often the port-tack boat can find a gap between the starboard tackers, and if she converges with one, she may be able to slow down, pass astern, and still beat the starboard tacker around the mark because of not having to come about. The starboard tacker will be cautious about tacking too close to the other boat (for fear of infringing rule 41.2), which may give a definite advantage to the port tacker. This situation is also explained in Figure 5-11.

When the mark is left to port, it is often too risky to try a port-tack approach if there is a crowd at the mark. The reason for this is that a tack under the lee bow of the approaching starboard tackers might mean that you cannot fetch, while going astern of the starboard tackers and coming about clear of their backwind obviously puts you behind. About all one can do with a port turn is try to get to the mark first, and if you can't, join the parade of starboard tackers a little above the lay line where you can get as much clear wind as possible. If there are boats approaching you on the port tack that might tack under your lee bow, it is possible to fake that you are not quite fetching by temporarily heading slightly below the mark and letting your sails luff a bit to give the impression that you are pinching. This may encourage the starboard tackers to pass astern of you and overstand. Don't bear off, however, when very close to the port tacker, as this could be considered balking.

Some aspects of steering and tacking downwind were discussed in Chapter 4, but the important matter of downwind
strategy in shifty winds has not yet been treated. A general
rule for running toward a leeward mark that is definitely not
dead downwind is to sail the boat on her optimim heading,
proceeding on the tack that brings her closest to the mark.
This strategy will give you the best odds for gains provided
factors such as current, variations in wind strength, and the
positions of competitors play no major part. Most sailors
know this rule, but they are often in considerable doubt about
which tack to take when the leeward mark is dead downwind.

If one has a reasonably good expectation of wind shift, a
good rule to follow is to take the tack that heads you away
from the direction of the shift. For example, if you are running before a northerly and expect a slight easterly veer, head
southwesterly on the optimal heading (for the most effective

FIGURE 5-12: CHOOSING THE DOWNWIND TACK

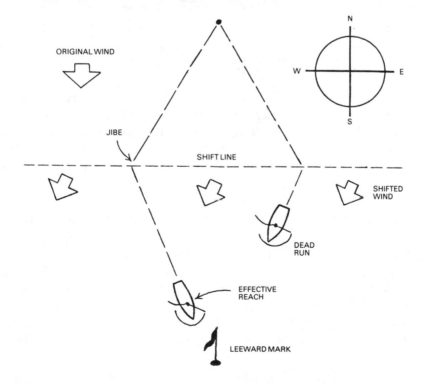

Alberg 30s racing. On this point of sailing it may pay to head high on the initial part of the leg so that a spinnaker can be set on the final part, or, vice versa, to sail low initially with the 'chute and then later head higher under the genoa. The strategy may depend on the point of sailing during the next leg. (Photograph, Bill Schill.)

drawing of your spinnaker), and when the easterly shift occurs, jibe over and head east of south. This is explained in Figure 5-12. Notice that the boat following the opposite strategy, sailing toward the southeast initially, gets the shifted wind from dead astern, and she will therefore be at a distinct disadvantage unless there is quite a fresh wind that allows her to run dead before it at top speed.

On a near beam-reaching course toward a turning mark, an old rule is to head low initially and then sharpen up (head higher) on the final part of the leg so that the boat will have more speed and control when approaching the mark. But this strategy will depend partly on expected changes in the wind. For instance, if the wind strength is expected to increase, it may pay to sail high initially for more speed and then sail lower after the wind has freshened (see the section on down-

FIGURE 5-13: ANTICIPATING THE NEXT LEG

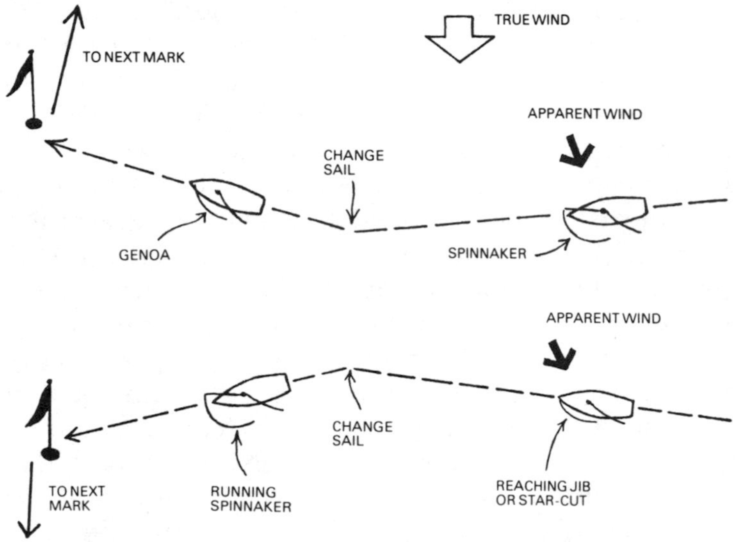

wind helmsmanship in Chapter 4). Another consideration is anticipating which sails will be carried on the next leg. If the leg will be a beat, you may want to sail low initially in order to carry the spinnaker effectively and then change to a genoa (or carry the 'chute with genoa) and head higher for the final approach to the mark. On the other hand, if the next leg will be a run it may pay to head high initially under a reaching jib (or star-cut) and then bear off for the mark so that a running 'chute can be set well in advance of reaching the mark. This is explained in Figure 5-13.

There are some subtle differences in strategy between a short race and a long one. Of course, general weather system forecasts have a somewhat different meaning and become more important for a long-distance ocean racer, but aside from that, there should be a slightly different approach in the manner of sailing. On a long race one should be less concerned with sailing the most direct course and more concerned with pure boat speed as opposed to speed made good. In other words, keep your boat moving at top speed whether or not you are sailing directly toward your destination. Of course, this is a sweeping generality, and there are important exceptions, such as when a weather forecast might dictate otherwise, but by and large the rule pays more often than not. The reason for this is that on a long race weather conditions are more likely to change to the overall benefit of the faster indirect course (provided the course is not too indirect). When the wind is on the nose, for example, a full-and-by course will generally pay over a slower pinching course, because a heading shift will put the pincher almost dead astern of a faster footing boat, while a significant lift may allow the footing boat to fetch.

When reaching or running, the same principle often applies. An indirect course that gives optimum speed, allowing best use of the spinnaker or other effective reaching sails, will get you far ahead of a competitor that can't make the best use of these sails. One shouldn't worry too much about getting away from the rhumb line (direct course) when far from the finish, because the chances are that the wind will shift later on. The overriding rule here is to use the wind you have to best advantage while you have it.

Some racing skippers make the mistake of not modifying their wardrobe of sails for distance races. For instance, it may be most advantageous to carry a large genoa jib on a short round-the-buoys race, but it could very well pay to carry a lower-rated, faster-reaching double-head rig (see Chapter 3) on an important ocean race. Of course, a genoa might be needed on a short beat to the finish. Generally speaking, the closer one is to the finish, the more the long-distance race takes on the characteristics of a short race.

When beating toward a finish or other mark that is nearby but out of sight, one must be careful not to overstand. I have made this mistake more than a few times. If you suspect that the wind will shift but are not sure which way or when, don't get too far from the present rhumb line. The closer you get to your destination, the closer you should stick to the rhumb line, unless perhaps there is a special advantage in working along a shore or unless you are trying to avoid extra tacking in light airs. Another reason for not getting very far from the rhumb line is that when the upwind mark is out of sight, you must depend on your navigation to know where you are in relation to the mark, and most forms of yacht navigation are seldom completely accurate.

The important matter of current has not yet been discussed (except in relation to the start), and this is an aspect of racing that is frequently misunderstood even by many veterans. The most common misconception seems to be that of a lee bow tide. I have heard old-timers speak with reverence of the lee bow effect, which is supposed to boost a boat to windward as a result of added hydrodynamic lift. In actuality, however, this is a myth; for if the current is uniform everywhere, all boats will be similarly affected by it. (There will, however, be a difference in how the current affects the apparent winds of the various boats when they are on entirely different headings.) In a situation where a boat beating full-and-by has the current on her windward bow but can be pinched up to bring the current on her lee bow, consideration should not be given to the lee bow effect. If the boat responds well to pinching she should be pinched, or if her Vmg is improved by footing she should be sailed full-and-by, but the current really has nothing to do with it.

On the other hand, when the current is not uniform in direction over the racing area, there is some real advantage to getting the flow on your lee bow. Uniformity of the current is often changed by the geography and topography of the land and bottom. For instance, points of land cause eddies, while deep channels and rivers flowing into larger bodies of water also can bend or distort the current. An effective strategy is often to tack toward the mouth of a river when the distortion of flow provides a push against the lee bow. A typical situation of this kind is illustrated in Figure 5-14.

Other effects of the current that seem much more obvious are also frequently disregarded or misinterpreted. Some sailors do not seem to realize that there are often great time differences in the turn of the current at different locations within a limited racing area. This may be due to the depth of water

FIGURE 5-14: LEE BOW EFFECT IN NONUNIFORM CURRENTS

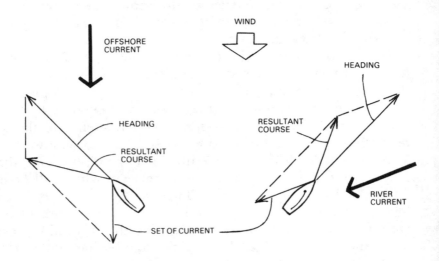

(current usually changes first over a shoal) or to geographical features of the land. Time differences are best determined by a study of local current charts and tidal current tables, and, of course, by keeping a record of observations.

Another mistake that is made with surprising frequency is to misjudge the sideways push of a beam current. Direction and velocity of flow can be obtained from current tables, but allowances have to be made for unusual tide and wind conditions. Careful note should be made of the current every time a mark is rounded, and, of course, any fixed objects that are passed close aboard such as lobster or crab pot buoys, anchored vessels, fishnet stakes, or navigation aids should also be observed to determine the flow. Once the direction and velocity of the current are known, the change of course necessary to compensate for the lateral push can be determined by drawing a simple vector on the chart, or lateral current tables can be used. Such tables are found under the heading "Coping with Currents" in the annual publication, *Eldridge Tide and Pilot Book*, and they tell how many degrees to change your course and also by what percentage your speed is decreased or increased, depending on whether the current is angled off the bow or stern. Obviously, a beam current will cause the greatest lateral movement, while a small angle will cause little movement to the side. The tables mentioned give the course and speed change for every 15 degrees of current angle, and the tables are entered with the ratio of boat speed to current speed.

A simple rule of thumb requiring no tables is the 60 formula. The length of the course in miles is divided into 60, and this figure is multiplied by the estimated distance a beam current will set you. The result is the number of degrees the course must be changed to compensate. For example, if you will be sailing east for 10 miles, and you figure the current will set you to the south by 2 miles, divide 10 into 60, multiply the resulting 6 by 2, and the resulting 12 gives you the number of degrees you must steer north of your heading to compensate for the current. This formula holds true only for a beam current, but lateral movement can be approximated for a current angle of 45 degrees by multiplying the 60 formula result by two-thirds, or a current angle of 30 degrees by multiplying the result by one-half.

I don't like to conclude this chapter with an overworked cliché, but any racing sailor interested in improving must bear in mind the old adage that practice makes perfect. In trying to analyze my own numerous mistakes over the years, I find that a great many have resulted from lack of practice in racing sail handling, close maneuvering, certain aspects of tuning, and working with and training the crew. It is not enough just to sail in a lot of races. The skipper and crew should have occasional practice sessions to develop and polish such maneuvers and skills as tacking, spinnaker handling, sail shaping, reefing, changing jibs, and even navigation.

Everyone on board should have a job and know what he is expected to do; and when mistakes are made, they should be analyzed methodically after the race. One (slight) compensation for losing races as a result of making mistakes is that there is always something to be learned from them. At least one prominent skipper has said that he learns more from losing than from winning.

6

Cruising Seamanship

Compared with the racer, the cruising sailor often sails short-handed, and his crew may not be so skilled; while compared with the daysailer, the cruiser spends more time in strange waters, and he is often away from familiar facilities and readily available help if it should be needed. Thus the value of avoiding mistakes while cruising should be obvious.

Below Deck

Fitting out a boat above deck was discussed in Chapter 1, but here we are concerned with mistakes in equipping a boat below deck—mistakes that can cause accidents or problems of one kind or another.

Surprisingly, many boat manufacturers do not recognize that a sailboat often heels beyond an angle of about 25 degrees. At least that is the way it seems. judging from the heights of fiddles and the security of locker doors. Fiddles or sea rails serve the important purpose of keeping objects from spilling out of shelves when the boat is heeled, and they should be high enough to provide security at considerable angles of heel, because any boat, even one sailing on sheltered waters, can be knocked down by a sudden puff or be rolled by a powerboat swell. Objects falling from shelves or lockers not only can be broken but also can become projectiles that could cause injury. For our boat's bookshelf, which runs fore-and-aft, we made a removable fiddle that has proven very satisfactory, and it is illustrated in Figure 6-1. The shock cord shown in the figure runs from the fiddle around behind the books and through a hole in the side of the shelf, and its purpose is to hold the books firmly and keep them from falling on their side. The knot on the outside of the shelf end can be adjusted so the shock cord will always hold the books tightly even when a number of them are removed. Fiddles of ample height should also be provided around counter tops and tables and anywhere else objects can fall or spill.

Lockers also can spill their contents very easily when the boat is heeled or in rough seas. Thus it is important that their doors be closed securely. All too frequently one sees such doors fitted with magnetic or friction latches, and these are all but worthless. Perhaps the best kind of latches are metal spring catches mounted inside the lockers and reached through round finger holes. However, be sure the reach holes are considerably larger than a person's finger, because a finger could be caught and broken in a small hole if the person opening the locker lost his balance in rough seas.

Drawers should be self-locking so that they cannot slide out when they are closed. This is usually accomplished with notched runner ends that lock on the lip of the drawer sill, and the closed drawer is simply lifted up slightly to unlock so that it can be opened (see Figure 6-2). In my opinion this arrangement is not all that is necessary for a short drawer, because it could slide all the way out when the drawer is being opened (with the locking notch not engaged). A falling drawer will not only spill its contents and possibly scar the woodwork, but it could injure a person's foot. One simple solution to the problem is to install a short drop pin through the back end of the bottom of the drawer. The pin will catch

FIGURE 6-1: FORE-AND-AFT BOOKSHELF

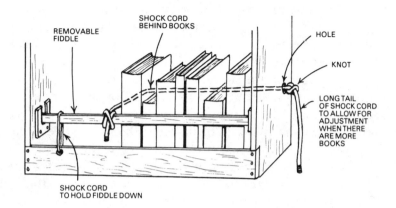

FIGURE 6-2: A SAFETIED DRAWER

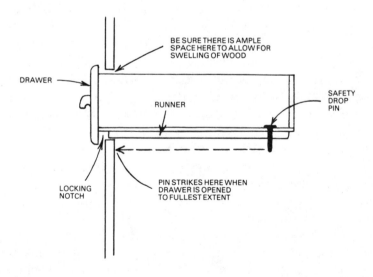

on the sill when the drawer is opened almost to its fullest extent. This is illustrated in Figure 6-2.

Most cruising boats I have been aboard do not have adequate bunk boards or similar arrangements to prevent the crew from being thrown or rolled out of their berths. Lack of these safeguards can and have caused serious injuries. For the roughest possible offshore work, I think automobile type seat belts provide the greatest security, but for ordinary cruising on soundings lee cloths will serve very well. These are rectangular cloths, usually made of dacron, about four feet long and a foot and a half high, securely fastened to the outboard edge of the bunks. Each cloth is held up with about three lines that attach to the overhead—perhaps to a handrail. Incidentally, adequate handrails are also important so that one can hang on in rough weather. Few stock boats have enough securely attached handrails or other grips below deck.

Corners of tables, counters, and low bulkheads are not always rounded, but they certainly should be if there is the slightest chance that someone could be thrown against them in heavy weather. Also, every boat on which cooking is done while standing up when underway needs a safety belt to support the cook so that he or she can work with both hands. Many boats are not so equipped, and when they are, the belts are usually the wrong design. Our galley belt was criticized several years ago by designer-ocean voyager John Letcher because it merely went around the cook's waist or bottom and had no strap in front to prevent the cook from being thrown into the stove. Now we have a front strap to hold the cook steady no matter which way the boat rolls or heels.

Of course, galley stoves need fiddles and/or clamps to hold pots, pans, and kettles on the burners. Most stoves are gimbaled but not always adequately. In my opinion gimbaling should allow the stove to remain level to at least a heeling angle of 35 degrees on *both* tacks. See that the stove has a remote shut-off valve or other means of closing off the fuel in the event that the entire stove should be afire. A fire extinguisher should be mounted in the galley area, but a frequent mistake is to mount it too close to the stove. Be sure that

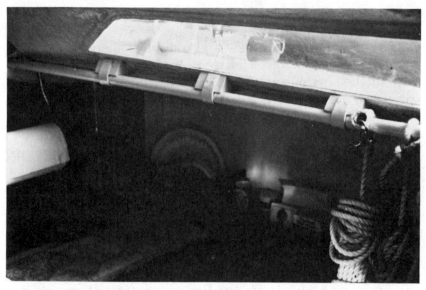

A clever arrangement on a Chance-designed Offshore One. The pipe secured beneath the window serves not only as a below-decks handrail for rough weather, but the pipe, and its twin on the opposite side of the boat, also serves as a conduit for the spinnaker foreguy and jib Cunningham in order that the deck can be kept free of excess lines. (Photograph, R. C. Henderson.)

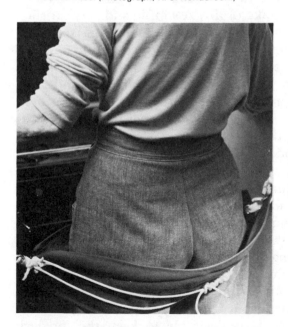

A proper galley belt. Notice that there is a strap in front as well as in back to keep the cook from being thrown against the stove. (Photograph, R. C. Henderson.)

burner controls are clearly marked to indicate when they are in the closed position.

Too many boats, both new and old, have fiberglass liners or wood ceilings that block accessibility to the interior of the hull shell. This means that the shell cannot be properly inspected or jury repaired from the inside in the event of collision and that wiring, piping, and fastenings cannot always be reached. In many cases there is not even proper accessibility to the entire bilge—a defect that prevents thorough cleaning, the clearing of limbers (drain holes), the tightening of keel bolts, and so forth. Quite often this condition can be rectified by cutting access holes and/or putting hatches in the cabin sole. In our boat two large access holes were fitted with doors so that the dead spaces were turned into useful lockers.

Lack of ventilation below deck can lead to severe mildew and rot (not to mention carbon monoxide poisoning when the engine is running). It is usually wise to install one or two extra ventilators and to cut ventilation holes in lockers or any dead air spaces. Dorades, which admit air but keep out spray and rain, are usually the most satisfactory permanent vents, but they do limit the intake of air. A simple and very satisfactory in-the-harbor arrangement I use on our boat is a large standard cowl vent facing forward and located on the foredeck where it can admit a strong flow of air into the forepeak. To keep water out, I simply hang a large plastic bucket under the hole as shown in Figure 6-3. The bucket is hung on a bent metal plate fastened to the deck plate bolts of the ventilator as illustrated. Of course, this is only a temporary rig for harbor or sheltered waters, and the bucket has to be emptied every so often. I have found, however, that it takes a surprisingly long period of continual rain to fill the bucket. In fact, I have never yet found the bucket filled completely, although I leave our boat for months at a time during the winter.

Another alternative that avoids the use of a large permanent Dorade box is the small PVC water trap such as the kind made by Nicro/Fico that can be used with a standard cowl vent (see Figure 6-3). This kind, like the Dorade, restricts the flow of air to some extent, but it allows easy removal for very heavy weather or when it is desirable to keep the foredeck clear.

FIGURE 6–3: VENTILATION WITHOUT PERMANENT DORADES

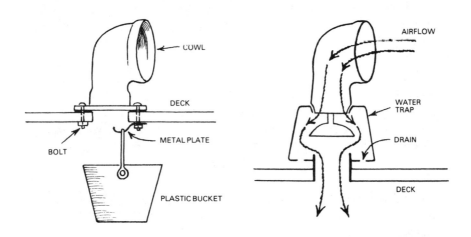

Speaking of keeping water out of the cabin, a great many small cruising boats lack a feature that is very important for comfort—a locker for foul weather gear near the companionway. Occasionally sailors come below in their wet foul weather gear and sit down on a bunk. Once the bunk has become wet with salt water, it will seldom be completely dry again, because the salt-impregnated mattress or bedding will absorb moisture from the air even on a sunny day if there is any humidity in the air. There should be a locker or space as close as possible to the companionway where wet gear can be hung or stowed as soon as the off-watch sailor comes below so water will not have to be tracked into the rest of the cabin.

Basic plumbing, piping, and electric wiring have been discussed in my books *Sea Sense* and *The Cruiser's Compendium*. Further details can be found in the American Boat and Yacht Council's book, *Safety Standards for Small Craft*. Here is a brief list of common failings for which the boat owner should be alert:

• Wiring improperly insulated and secured or installed insufficiently high above the bilge so that it could get wet during a knockdown.

• Wiring stretched too tight so that it doesn't allow for normal hull flexing and chafe.

• Battery and master switch installed inside engine compartment where they are not readily accessible and where excessive heat may impair performance and accelerate deterioration of the batteries.

• Improper battery box without a lid or battery box that is not adequately ventilated.

• Undersize wiring that is improperly fused.

• Copper piping without flexible hose connections to protect against metal fatigue from vibration.

• Insufficient hose clamps (use two together wherever possible).

• Lack of seacocks where pipes or hoses penetrate the hull or the use of cheap brass gate valves that are likely to corrode and fail.

• Seacocks out of easy reach.

• Tanks inadequately secured or insufficiently baffled and water tanks lacking adequate access holes for cleaning.

• Tank air vents located where they can admit spray or rain (water tank vent pipes can terminate below deck, but fuel tank vents must be above deck in a protected location with the vent pipe bent into a loop or swan neck to keep water out).

• Head bowl (toilet) located below load waterline (its rim should be at least a few inches above the waterline to prevent overflow in case a check valve should fail when the seacocks are open).

• Head discharge hose not looped and vented to prevent back-siphoning when the boat is heeled.

• Head discharge outlet forward of the intake (this allows the discharge to be pumped back into the head).

• Holding tanks improperly secured.

• Sinks located too far away from the boat's centerline where they can admit sea water and overflow when the boat heels (such sinks should be fitted not only with seacocks but also with good watertight drain stoppers).

• Lack of check valves in the low points of fresh water lines supplying sinks (these valves hold water in the lines and avoid the need of excessive pumping to clear the lines of air).

• Lack of water traps in the icebox drain that will prevent cold air from escaping (if possible there should be a dip in the line to trap water and thus block the escape route for sinking cold air).

• Lack of sumps for ice water and bilgewater (no corrective measures can be taken if the bilges are flat and there is a solid fin keel that bolts to the bottom of the boat).

• Inadequate limbers in the bilge (any areas in the bilge and interior of the topsides that can trap water should have drains sufficiently large to discourage clogging).

• Drains in lockers where LP-gas cylinders are stored subject to being clogged by any loose gear that is stowed in the lockers. Be sure there is a coarse raised screen to keep gear away from drains so that in the improbable event of a gas leak the gas will always flow overboard.

Anchoring and Docking

Cruising on soundings obviously involves a great deal of anchoring and/or docking, and these activities create problems that are not always handled in the best manner. Some of the most common anchoring mistakes are anchoring in the wrong spot; carrying ground tackle that is too light; using the wrong kind of anchor; mismatching the anchor and rode; throwing rather than lowering the anchor overboard; paying out the rode before the boat has sternway; failing to snub the rode to be sure the anchor has dug in; paying out insufficient scope; using a trip line and buoy improperly; failing to use two anchors when they are needed; providing insufficient protection from chafe; and breaking out the anchor improperly.

Many of these points need elaboration. In selecting a spot to anchor, of course, you want a windward shore that affords protection, water sufficiently deep to avoid grounding at low tide, and the best possible holding bottom. Furthermore, you want to be as far as possible from other boats so that there will be ample swinging room with sufficient scope. Perhaps the most unusual breach of seamanship is for one boat to anchor too close to another. It should be realized that scope is the radius of an arc of swing when the boat is moved by a shift of wind or current (see Figure 6-4, A) and all boats do not swing exactly the same way simultaneously. Some sail around on their rodes or yaw a great deal, while other boats remain relatively docile, and their movement is slower. Behavior at anchor will depend on such factors as displacement, freeboard, rig, and type of keel. If swinging room is very limited and your boat is a natural "swinger" or if there is a lot of tidal current, you should use two anchors.

To inhibit yawing, a method loosely referred to as the hammerlock moor is often effective (see Figure 6-4, B). One simple way of using this system is to drop the primary anchor in the normal way; pay out ample scope (at least five times the depth of water); and then wait for the boat to yaw. At the end of the most extreme yaw, drop a second (usually lighter) anchor; pay out just enough scope for it to dig in when the boat swings back; then shorten scope somewhat on the primary anchor. A still better way, when one has the room to do it, is to drop the primary anchor and then move the boat (under power or sail) at right angles to the direction of the wind or current that will control the anchored boat. When almost at the end of your scope, drop the secondary anchor and pay out scope until the boat drifts downwind (or down current) to a position where the two rodes make an angle to each other of about 90 degrees as illustrated in Figure 6-4, B. Of course, another way of putting out a second anchor is by rowing it out in the dinghy after the primary anchor has been set, and this is sometimes the easiest way to get a wide angle between the two rodes when the skipper fails to realize initially that two anchors will be needed. If swinging room is very limited or if there is a strong current that alternates in opposite directions, a recommended system is the Bahamian moor, in which two anchors are put out in opposite directions in such a way that the boat rides to one hook on an ebb current and the other hook on a flood (see Figure 6-4, C). One problem associated with this mooring method is that the rode leading astern will sometimes foul on a deep fin keel. However, this difficulty can usually be overcome by attaching weights to the rodes to hold them down when they are not under strain as shown in the illustration.

FIGURE 6-4: ANCHORING

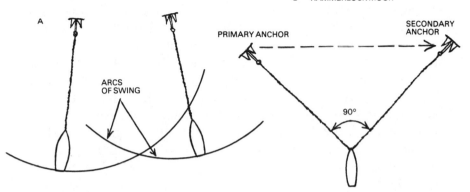

A

ARCS
OF SWING

B   HAMMERLOCK MOOR

PRIMARY ANCHOR

SECONDARY
ANCHOR

90°

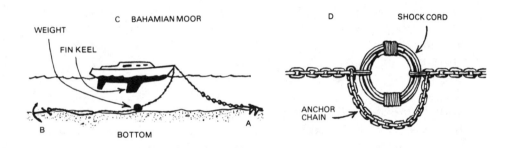

C   BAHAMIAN MOOR

WEIGHT

FIN KEEL

B

BOTTOM

A

D

SHOCK CORD

ANCHOR
CHAIN

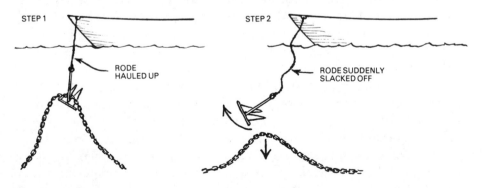

E   CLEARING A FOULED DANFORTH

STEP 1

RODE
HAULED UP

STEP 2

RODE SUDDENLY
SLACKED OFF

There is a lot of controversy concerning the proper kind, size, and weight of ground tackle, but there is little doubt that many sailors carry the wrong gear. As a general rule, you should carry at least three anchors on a cruising boat: a lunch hook, a working anchor, and a storm anchor. Also, you should carry a variety of types that will be suitable for every type of seabed you could possibly encounter. Many boats carry different size anchors of the same type but then the best possible hook for every type of bottom is not available. For instance, Hi-Tensile Danforths and CQR plow types are ideal for sand, mud, and sticky clay; but a hooking anchor such as the yachtsman or grapnel is best for rock, coral, or heavily weeded bottoms.

Some sailors believe that for storm conditions two working anchors are satisfactory, but I am convinced that it is better to use one heavy storm anchor with ample scope. Two anchors are fine to restrict swinging and for use in alternating opposed currents, but in very heavy weather they will often take the strain alternately rather than simultaneously and consequently drag, one at a time. Furthermore, entanglements are possible, and if the rodes differ in scope and the two anchors drag in line (one directly behind the other), the near anchor may cut a trough that weakens the holding power of the other.

One of the greatest controversies concerning ground tackle is the weight of the anchor and the size of the rode. One school of thought advocates relatively lightweight anchors used with light nylon rode, the theory being that light nylon is stretchier than heavy and thus reduces shock loading. While there is some logic in this thinking, it is risky when carried to the extreme. Lightweight Hi-Tensile Danforth anchors have tremendous holding power when well dug in, but they often need a certain amount of weight to make them dig in when the bottom is less than ideal. Furthermore, the size of the rode should not be determined only by its dry breaking strength. Authorities on rope say that nylon loses up to 20 percent of its strength when wet, and it must have sufficient diameter to resist surface wear, industrial pollution, and deterioration from exposure to ultraviolet rays from the sun. Additionally, a rode should be thick enough to grip firmly with the hands, and it should last. Light rodes must be replaced much more often.

In *The Expert's Book of Boating* Raymond E. Miskelly, a director of reasearch for a major cordage company, writes that "ropes in the smaller sizes need replacing more frequently since all the yarns in the smaller rope sizes are subject to surface wear. In larger ropes, which contain center yarns in the strands, the inner fibers are protected from surface abrasion, which increases their life and the limit of safety of the rope before replacement becomes necessary." He goes on to say, "It should be kept in mind that repeated overloading will greatly reduce rope life. A factor of safety of 5 to 1 should be allowed with new rope, and remember that the margin of safety decreases as the rope wears. In selecting the rope size, it is far better to err on the high side than to try to get along with a small size." Miskelly recommends nylon anchor rode of considerably greater diameter than what is usually carried.

As for the problem of elasticity, medium-diameter nylon rope will stretch considerably with sufficient scope. When scope must be limited a "rubber snubber" can be used; it holds a bight of slack in the rode, allowing the elastic rubber strap to take the strain. One word of warning, however—be very cautious about using the type of snubber that is attached to the rode by weaving the line through three holes in each end of the snubber, because I have heard that these can cause serious chafe. The rode might be tied to the snubber, but it is usually better to lash the snubber to the rode. When elasticity is limited, obviously the anchor must be heavier.

Many veteran sailors prefer chain rather than rope for the rode. With sufficient scope, chain supplies shock absorption through its catenary (sag), but at short scope it can easily jerk loose a light anchor, especially in rough water. When lack of swinging room severely limits scope, an elastic shock absorber becomes very important. A rubber snubber will fill the bill, or one can use a coil of shock cord as illustrated in Figure 6-4, D. Not only will the shock cord supply elasticity, but the circular coil will help absorb the shock loading as it elongates. My favorite rode is a medium-sized nylon line (used with a medium-weight anchor) with a short length of chain (I have a piece ten feet long and another thirty feet) between the rope and the anchor. The short chain adds weight to the anchor, prevents the line from chafing on the bottom, and makes a catenary that is helpful to shock absorption. Many sailors use this system, but I don't think the short chain is always long enough.

Several points should be made concerning anchoring technique. Some small-boat sailors *throw* out their anchors, but in deep water where one cannot see the bottom this is risky because of the possibility that the anchor will be fouled by its rode. The anchor should be lowered gently as the boat moves backward to assure that the rode cannot become entangled with the flukes or stock. Also, many sailors simply lower their anchor, pay out scope, and assume that the hook will hold. One should make sure the flukes dig in, and this is accomplished only by backing away from the anchor (or moving ahead with the rode leading aft) and then snubbing. Don't back up unnecessarily fast, however, as this could (and has) caused difficulties for the person handling the rode, allowing tangles and even pinched fingers.

Anchor trip lines are often needed when there is risk of snagging the flukes under rocks or chains lying on the bottom. Buoyed trip lines, however, can be fouled by other boats or even by one's own boat under certain tide and current conditions. One simple way to avoid this problem is to use a short trip line, a little longer than the depth of water at high tide, secured in the usual way to the crown of the anchor and with the other end of the line secured as far as it will reach up the anchor rode. This allows the hauling end of the trip line to be reached when the rode is pulled up at short stay. Incidentally, sailors do not always realize that a Danforth anchor hooked on a chain can often be cleared without a trip line by simply hauling the chain well up off the bottom and then quickly slacking the rode. This will cause the anchor to drop but glide forward a bit, allowing the chain to slip off (see Figure 6-4, E). The method may all also work with a plow anchor.

As nearly everyone knows, breaking out the hook is normally accomplished at short stay (with the rode nearly straight up and down) by driving the boat ahead. Sometimes, however, the anchor can be broken out by backing down or even circling around it. A particularly stubborn hook that is deeply buried may be loosened by keeping crew weight forward while the rode is winched in sufficiently to pull the bow down. Then the crew moves aft while the boat is alternately driven ahead and backed under power. A couple of times my wife and I have lifted stubborn anchors from the stern of our dinghy. We pull the rode up sufficiently taut to put the stern down, and then we move to the bow and proceed to jump up and down until the anchor works loose.

Docking a cruising boat, of course, requires complete familiarity with the way one's boat behaves under power. Most modern auxiliary sailboats are cut away forward below the waterline, and this feature, together with windage forward, causes the bow to blow off at low speed, especially when backing. Failure to take this into consideration often leads to docking difficulties. For instance, the bow line may not be secured soon enough when landing at the leeward side of the dock, and the line is sometimes let go too soon when backing away from the dock. With sufficient crew it is often a good idea to stop headway and swing the boat into the dock with a spring line rigged from amidships leading aft, but most sailboats are not fitted with proper amidships cleats or chocks. It may be possible to use a block attached to the rail with the line led to a winch, but one must be careful to see that the block is amply strong and properly swiveled and that the point of attachment is solid.

A common mistake when docking is not taking the bow and stern lines far enough forward and aft. Those lines should be cleated on the dock far ahead of and behind the boat to allow for the rise and fall of the tide. Another error that has frequently been pointed out (but is still committed nevertheless) is to put the eye of your docking line over a bollard or piling so that it lies on top of a line belonging to a neighboring boat. This means that your neighbor cannot cast off without first removing your line. The way to avoid the problem is to run your eye splice or knotted loop up through the neighbor's eye before your line is dropped over the bollard as shown in Figure 6-5, A. Then either line may be cast off without disturbing the other.

One of the most difficult docking operations is the so-called Mediterranean moor, which requires one to drop a bow anchor and back into a space between two boats. I must admit that my experience with this maneuver is very limited, but a most experienced skipper, R. J. Brandon, described a method in a letter to *Yachting Monthly* magazine (August 1974) that appears to be very sensible and which Brandon claims has always worked for his thirty-six-foot auxiliary cruiser. The method, illustrated in Figure 6-5, B, begins with a bow-first approach under power (boat position 1) for the purpose of securing a bow line ashore (boat position 2). Then the boat is backed out of the space while the bow line is payed out until the stern can be turned into the wind clear of the neighboring boats (position 3). Next, the engine is driven ahead and the boat is turned into a position at which a bow anchor can be dropped exactly between the anchors of her neighbors (position 4). Meanwhile, the line leading ashore has been transferred to the stern, and the stern is pulled toward the shore while the anchor rode is paid out (position 5). It probably will not be necessary to use the engine in reverse while the boat is being backed into her berth. Keeping some tension on the rode while the stern is being pulled ashore will keep the boat from drifting down on the neighbor to leeward. My illustration differs only slightly from the one appearing in *Yachting Monthly,* the only significant difference being that my line ashore is secured close to the windward neighbor (rather than in the middle of the berth) so as to help keep the boat away from the leeward neighbor as her stern is being pulled toward the shore. Of course, the line put ashore must be a long one. The light rode for the lunch hook should do.

FIGURE 6–5: DOCKING PROBLEMS

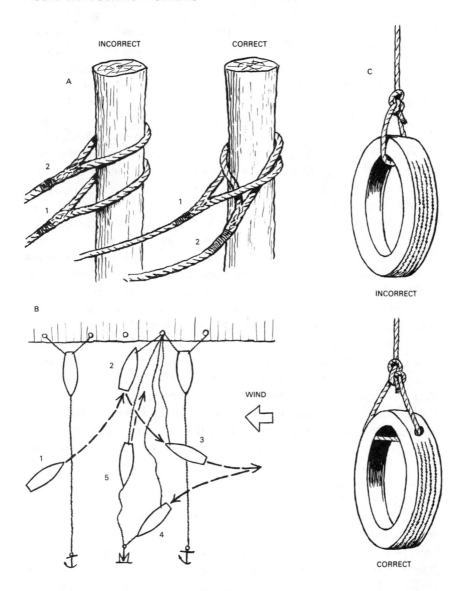

Sometimes it may be necessary to turn a boat around under power between two docks that are rather close together, and the turning must be done by alternately reversing and going ahead. The proper technique for the usual cruiser, one having her propeller just forward of her rudder, is to go ahead with short bursts of power so that water is pushed against one side of the turned rudder, pushing the stern away from the side toward which the rudder is turned. It is not always realized that it is not necessary to reverse the helm when backing alternately. Reversing the helm only wastes valuable time, because the kind of boat under discussion cannot be steered backward unless she is making considerable speed in reverse. In other words, you cannot "kick" the stern to one side in reverse, because the prop wash is not directed against the rudder. To make a quick and tight port turn, for instance, turn the rudder hard to port, kick the stern to starboard with a quick burst of power ahead, reverse briefly without changing the rudder, kick ahead again, reverse briefly, and so forth.

Cruising often involves rafting, the lashing of one or more boats to a boat that is at anchor. Of course, the anchored boat must have ground tackle substantial enough to hold all the boats, and there should be an equal number of boats on either side of the anchored one whenever possible. A common accident is to get spreaders locked when coming alongside. Always look aloft when landing at a raft, and lash your boat (with spring lines and a bow and stern line) so that your spreaders are abaft or forward of your neighbor's. Many people remain rafted all night, but this is really asking for trouble. The safest policy is for the raft to break up and each boat to put out its own anchor before the crew turn in.

Rafting and docking require abundant fenders. When cruising offshore, I normally carry a small automobile tire for use as a sea anchor, and this also makes a good heavy-weather fender when alongside a rough quay wall. But don't make the mistake I once made of putting the securing line around the tire the wrong way. I intended to use the tire only temporarily and so hung it in the manner shown by the sketch labeled "Incorrect" in Figure 6-5, C. The line chafed through in a surprisingly short time. A better way to support the tire is by cutting or boring holes at right angles to the tread and threading the support line through them as shown by the sketch labeled "Correct." Obviously this will eliminate chafe on the line. Some readers may not like the idea of carrying an ugly tire aboard, but I carry it lashed flat on the cabin top (with drain holes in the underside of the tire) and hidden by a neatly fitted cover. It is quite inoffensive, and I am comforted by knowing that I have a good drogue and sea anchor (when it is towed on end from a bridle), and an inexpensive heavy-duty fender as well.

Under Cruising Sail

Sails in general have already been discussed, but some points should be made concerning sails intended only for cruising. To begin with, I think the cruising sailor has a right to expect first-rate quality from the sailmaker. Too often cruisers are willing to accept poor-setting sails that the racer would never tolerate. All sails should have suitable draft without ridges, puckering, and hard spots; and they should be strongly constructed with proper reinforcing patches, chafe patches, and double stitching on heavy-weather sails. However, there are some minor differences between racing and true cruising sails. The latter should be made of softer material without resin filler so they will be easier to handle and stow. Unfilled sails take up about half the stowage room of those that are filled. Also, a sail used only for cruising should not have the same roach as a racing sail. An extreme roach is simply a way of obtaining extra unrated sail area, and it makes the leech difficult to control. Of course, the cruiser is not concerned with measurement rules, and normally all the sail area that will be needed can be obtained from increasing luff and foot lengths and headsail overlap.

It is also true that the cruiser need not be restricted by the number and length of battens. In my opinion it is often advisable for a ketch or yawl to carry full-length battens on the mizzen to minimize the effect of mainsail backwind. It is a good idea to have chafing strips sewn on mainsails or mizzens

A good genoa for short-handed cruising. The genoa on this Pearson 35 is powerful but not too large, and the head pendant can be removed to allow a tack pendant that will raise the foot for improved visibility and clearance of the lifelines.

where these sails lie against shrouds and spreaders when the booms are broad off. I wouldn't recommend that this be done on racers, however, because unless the sewing job is perfect (and quite often it is not), the strips will cause a slight amount of tightness or puckering of the sailcloth that may detract somewhat from the fairness of the camber.

Chafe prevention does not always receive the attention it should. Perhaps the most overlooked piece of equipment on a cruising boat is the boom vang. Of course, the device is constantly used aboard racing boats, but it is needed on cruisers also, primarily to alleviate chafe. A well-bowsed vang will hold the boom steady and help keep the sail from rubbing against the rigging. Regarding cruising headsails, I think the luff should be a little less than maximum length so that a short tack pendant can be used to raise the foot slightly for the sake of improving visibility and preventing the foot from chafing on the lifelines forward. Carrying a deck-sweeping jib on a cruising boat, especially one that is sailed short-handed, is an unnecessary risk because of the possibility of collision.

Self-steering is now beginning to catch on in the United States; but many cruising sailors still do not fully realize the advantage of being able to leave the helm unattended for at least short periods; nor do they realize how simple it is to make a well-balanced boat steer herself. Expensive and complicated vane gears are usually not necessary except perhaps for extended ocean passages made short-handed. Quite often simple sheet-to-helm connections will serve very well, and even long passages have been made very easily with such arrangements.

My favorite rig, which requires no special sails, is to secure the jib sheet to the windward side of the tiller and balance the pull of the jib with a piece of shock cord on the leeward side of the tiller as illustrated in Figure 6-6, A. Notice that the sheet is led from its winch across the cockpit to a block on the windward coaming and thence to the tiller, while the shock cord leads from the tiller to the leeward cockpit coaming. In light to moderate winds there is usually no need to put a turn of the sheet around its winch, but in strong winds with a large jib a turn may be desirable. The rig works best when sailing between a quartering and beam reach with the jib trimmed a little flatter than normal so that it is partially stalled. When the boat strays off course by turning into the wind the airflow becomes attached and the jib pulls harder, pulling the helm up and correcting the course; but when the boat turns downwind the jib loses power, allowing the shock cord to pull the tiller down, thus correcting the course.

With wheel steering, a drum bolted to the wheel, such as the one illustrated in Figure 6-6, B, may be used. I have one make by Marine Vane Gears in Cowes, England. Another possibility if the wheel works very freely is to use the emergency tiller, but the chances are that friction will be too great for the best results. With wheel steering or an emergency tiller rigged backward as shown in Figure 6-6, C, of course, the jib sheet will be led to the leeward side of the helm and the shock cord will be to windward as illustrated (the reverse of the way the sheet and shock cord are rigged for normal tiller steering).

When close-reaching, I can usually get our boat to sail herself well enough by simply readjusting the trim of the sails. Usually the jib is trimmed a bit flatter than normal and the mainsheet is eased slightly, depending on what headsail is up. Under difficult conditions (with puffy wind or bad seas) I sometimes set up a very simple wind vane, a QME (Quantock Marine Enterprises) gear that was described in *The Cruiser's Compendium.* Another, simpler alternative for close-reaching (or points considerably further off the wind) is to set a small staysail inside the jib (Figure 6-6, D). The staysail is backed slightly and its windward sheet is led through blocks to the windward side of the tiller, while shock cord is rigged to the tiller's leeward side to counterbalance the pull of the staysail (with wheel steering, of course, the rigging of the sheet and shock cord would be reversed). Should the boat head up, the sheet will pull harder than the shock cord and thus correct the helm; but if the boat bears off, the sheet will pull less hard and the shock cord will make the helm correction.

There are other relatively simple methods of making a boat steer herself. Some of these are discussed in my book *Single-handed Sailing,* but for a more technical look at the subject, I suggest a copy of John Letcher's book *Self-Steering for Sailing Craft.* For many years I was a slave to the helm before I realized how easy it can be to rig a well-balanced boat for self-steering. Of course, most avid sailors, including myself, usually enjoy steering, but there are certainly many times when it's a relief to leave the helm for short periods of time.

Sailing dead downwind is always a difficult problem, because the jib is blanketed by the mainsail. Carrying the spinnaker may be a partial solution, but quite often the short-handed cruiser does not want to expend the effort or risk the difficulties that are possible with the 'chute. The usual way to avoid blanketing the jib is to "wing it out" or carry it swung out on the side opposite the main, with or without a pole. Some sailors do not have the knack of sailing with a "wung-out" jib when it is not on a pole. As said in Chapter 4, the most effective method is to sail slightly by the lee, for then the sail will remain filled (see Figure 6-7, A). The trick is, of course, not to sail so far by the lee that the mainsail will jibe.

FIGURE 6-6: SIMPLE SELF-STEERING

From *Singlehanded Sailing,* published by International Marine Publishing Company

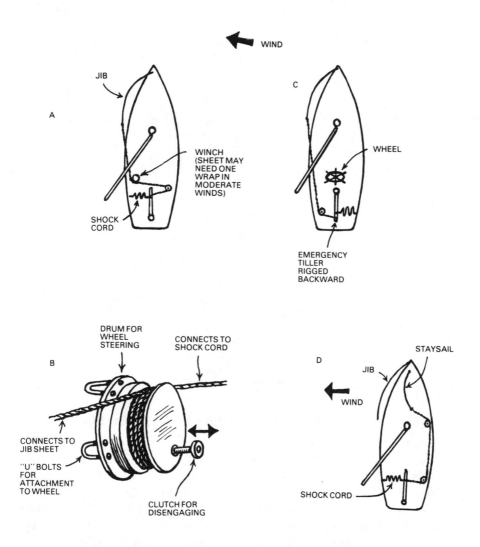

The helmsman must keep in a narrow groove between the point at which the mainsail begins to jibe and the point at which the jib starts to collapse. Again, be sure to rig a preventer to keep the main from jibing accidentally.

FIGURE 6-7: WINGING OUT THE JIB

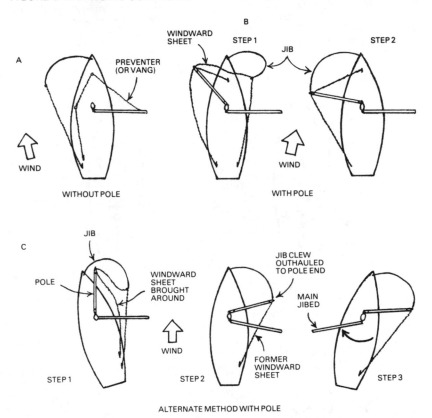

ALTERNATE METHOD WITH POLE

It is much easier to sail with the jib poled out, but difficulties are often encountered when setting up the rig in a breeze. I think the easiest method is to outhaul the sail (see Figure 6-7, B). First the spinnaker pole is set up to windward with a lift and foreguy as if it were being rigged for the 'chute. The windward sheet of the jib is run through the outboard end fitting of the pole (the way the spinnaker guy is usually rigged). The foreguy is tensioned enough to keep the pole off the forward shroud, and then the sheet is hauled (or winched) until the jib clew is pulled close to the pole end. In lighter winds the foreguy may not be necessary, for the leeward jib sheet might be tensioned to hold the pole steady. It is usually best to use a long-luff jib with little overlap, since the normal spinnaker pole is no longer than the base of the foretriangle. Of course, a boat that is never raced need not conform to racing rules and can have a considerably longer pole and thus satisfactorily wing out a jib with a much longer foot.

An alternate method of winging out in heavy weather is to pole the jib out to leeward in the lee of the main and then jibe the main to get the jib on the windward side. However, this method will obviously necessitate changing the heading of the boat somewhat. Sometimes the pole can be clipped to the load-carrying leeward sheet, but at other times it may be easier to bring the windward sheet around to leeward and run it through the pole end as illustrated by the alternate method shown in Figure 6-7, C.

Navigation
The discussion of navigation is really beyond the scope of this book, but a few of the most common mistakes in ordinary piloting should be mentioned. The most usual error is probably failure to carry sufficient updated charts. Many sailors, including myself, keep the same charts year after year, but this is a bad practice, for channels can change, markers are replaced, lights or numbers are changed, and sometimes new obstructions appear. Also, charts must be *used*. Many times uninformed or overconfident sailors steer directly from buoy to buoy without referring to the chart. Quite often this practice will work, but sometimes it will not, because channels may twist or curve and have unmarked shoals extending beyond a line between buoys. Incidentally, it is surprising how few cruising skippers get the *Notice to Mariners,* which tells of all important changes in information relating to safe navigation. These weekly publications can be obtained from the U.S. Coast Guard or the Defense Mapping Agency Hydrographic Center (DMAHC) in Washington, D.C.

Another occasional cause of piloting errors is confusion of the buoyage system. Some variations of the standard United States system occur on western rivers, intracoastal waterways, and in areas where state markers are used. Also, foreign waters

The navigator at work. It is highly recommended that every cruising boat except perhaps the very smallest have a navigator's niche and chart table. Proper organization of charts, instruments, and work area can help avoid navigation errors. (Photograph courtesy of Yacht Yard Sales.)

may be marked with a system almost directly opposite to that used in the United States. One must be careful, for instance, when cruising between various islands belonging to different countries in the West Indies. Details of the aids to navigation can be found in *List of Lights and Other Marine Aids (Light Lists)* and *Aids to Marine Navigation of the United States,* published by the U.S. Coast Guard; *U.S. Coast Pilots,* published by the National Ocean Survey; and *Sailing Directions* (pilots for foreign waters) published by the DMAHC. Of course, charts, chart books, and cruising guides also explain the channel markers and buoys.

Cruising guides, which give detailed written and pictorial descriptions of the cruising grounds, are usually carried by sailors venturing any distance from their home ports. However, don't consider these books as absolute gospel unless perhaps they have been published or reprinted very recently. Even a current publication date (printed on the cover or on one of the front pages) does not guarantee complete accuracy, because material for the book may have been gathered many months or a year or more before publication. Directions and suggestions in the cruising guides should be carefully noted, but always bear in mind that there could be changes in local channel markers, ranges, landmarks, facilities, and so forth.

Many newcomers to night sailing become very disoriented and confused when looking for aids to navigation against a background of shore lights. The important thing is to learn the exact characteristics of the lights you are looking for (from the chart and/or *Light List*) and to time their flashes accurately. A stopwatch or a wrist watch with a second hand is helpful, although some sailors manage well enough by counting: "one one thousand, two one thousand," and so on. One has to be sure he is not dragging or racing the beat too much when counting.

Be sure the binnacle light is not too bright and that the bulb has a red coating so that it will not blind the helmsman. For the same reason, see that no bright lights are turned on in the cabin, especially any that are in the helmsman's line of sight. It takes quite a while for the eyes to readjust to the darkness after they have been blinded by a strong light. Of course, a good pair of night binoculars can be invaluable.

Some inexperienced sailors have trouble judging the courses of ships at night, but this should not be a problem when one understands how the navigation lights are arranged. Bear in mind that if you see both a red and a green light it must mean the other vessel is approaching you head-on or almost so, but if you can see either the red or the green alone, then it means the vessel is more broadside-on. Ships have additional white range lights, and these give a more precise and easily visible angle of heading. A forward masthead range light directly under an after range light indicates the ship is headed directly at you, but when the lights spread apart the ship has turned or at least is not coming so directly toward you. The farther apart the range lights spread, the more oblique the course (the farther from you the ship has turned). Details of lighting for various vessel are explained in the nautical Rules of the Road. Every cruising boat should carry a copy of the rules that apply to the waters on which she sails (International, Inland, Great Lakes, or Western Rivers).

Undoubtedly the greatest piloting problems occur in fog. Needless to say, in any conditions of poor visibility a reliable compass is absolutely essential. Installation of the compass was discussed briefly in Chapter 1, but a few more points should be made concerning deviation.. Before cruising in waters that are subject to fog, it is most important to see that the compass is adjusted (corrected for deviation errors), preferably by a professional adjuster. Also, the skipper should constantly check his compass with bearings on buoys, landmarks, and ranges. Some years ago, during a cruise in Maine, I remember checking the compass by lining up two buoys just before we entered a fog bank. It turned out that the compass on our chartered boat was nearly 15 degrees off for our recently changed heading, and had we not made allowances for this inaccuracy, we could have hit some submerged rocks.

Many sailors, including myself, are careless about placing gear that can cause deviation near the compass. I have noticed that some of the newer boats are fitted with holders for drinking glasses on their binnacle pedestals, and these are a tempting place for small beer cans that may affect the compass. Also, some pedestals have winch handle holders, which may be all right if the handles are nonmagnetic, but certain kinds of stainless steel are magnetic. I had a demonstration of this fact when I bought an expensive, unbreakable, stainless steel thermos jug that was often placed near the helm during night watches. It turned out that the jug did have some effect on the compass. Other culprits are portable radios and light meters, which can cause considerable deviation. Incidentally, steel eyeglasses frames may also have some effect when the wearer uses a hand-bearing compass.

In addition to a reliable compass, an important requirement for fog piloting is an accurate method of determining distance run. If the boat is moving fast enough, a taffrail log towed far astern will probably give the greatest accuracy, but some electronic logs with underwater sensors projecting through the hull, such as the impeller types, are reasonably accurate. It is important, however, to test the accuracy in a variety of conditions.For instance, if the impeller is mounted on one side of the boat, the speed of water flow may be somewhat different on each tack. It has been said that impeller-type speedometer-logs are more reliable at low speeds when they are electrically powered externally rather than being self-powered by the turn of the impeller. If the boat is under power and she has no speedometer or log, a definite assist in determining speed is a tachometer, which gives the revolutions per minute of the engine. One must, of course, learn and note from experience just how fast the boat will go at various rpm's and in different conditions of wind and sea.

Many experienced sailors who are intimately familiar with their boats can reasonably well estimate speed through the water when the wind is fairly steady. Others who are not so gifted and who sail without speed or distance recording instruments can use what is commonly called a Dutchman's log, which is a floating object that is thrown overboard and timed as it passes between the bow and the stern. About the simplest way of using this method is to put a mark (a piece of tape perhaps) on the rail near the bow and another near the stern with a distance in even feet between the marks. A stopwatch is used to tell how many seconds it takes for the floating object to pass between the two marks. This time (in seconds) is divided into six-tenths (actually .592) times the distance between the marks, and the result gives a close approximation of speed in knots. Another way of stating it is: distance multiplied by three and divided by five times the number of seconds equals knots of speed.

Even when one can accurately determine his heading and distance run, it is possible to become lost in a fog, and this is usually due to unpredicted currents. Of course, the current should be figured from the tables, and more important, the actual flow of water should be noted when passing buoys, lobster pots, and so forth. When there are no stationary objects by which to judge the flow, however, the current can usually be determined by sounding with the lead line or preferably by anchoring. Obviously, the anchor will hold the boat stationary, and she will often lie bow into the current unless there is a strong wind, in which case the current can be judged by watching the flow around the hull. Sometimes it is possible to anchor small expendable floats in order to observe the drift of the boat. I read about one sailor who carries a bag of balloons for this purpose. They are anchored with pieces of string (a little longer that the water's depth) attached to nails or screws.

Three instruments useful for fog piloting that are not really exorbitant in price are the fathometer (depth sounder), radio direction finder, and Whistler Radar. I have never used the latter but have heard very good reports of it. The Whistler is a portable radar that is audible rather than visual. The operator scans the horizon with the instrument and listens for a sound echo over a pair of earphones. The distance away and the nature of the target can be determined by pitch variations in the return signal. Range is said to be up to about two miles. Complete information can be obtained from the manufacturer, Kimball Products, Inc., 60 Union Avenue, Sudbury, Massachusetts 01776.

Almost every cruising boat has (or should have) an RDF. This is a very useful tool, especially in foggy weather, but some sailors erroneously consider it a precision instrument for taking bearings. It serves well for homing but is not always reliable for obtaining an accurate fix from cross bearings. The reason is that the system has certain inherent inaccuracies such as the difficulty of finding the exact center of a null (minimum signal) and properly aligning the bearing scale, linear distance error (which increases with distance from a station), coastal refraction (land effect), polarization error (night effect), and RDF deviation.

Few sailors seem to pay much attention to RDF deviation, but it can have a significant effect on accuracy, especially when the bearings are broad on the bow or stern. The greatest deviation problem may be lifelines and stanchions if they interconnect to form a closed continuity of metal. Insulators are usually very helpful, but be sure they are the fail-safe type that, in the event of failure, allow the lifelines to remain connected. Plastic tubing makes a good substitute for standard manufactured insulators, and as suggested in Chapter 1, lashing the ends of the lifelines will help with this problem and afford a quick way of dropping the lines during an emergency without the need of pelican hooks, which are not always reliable. The RDF set should always be operated in the same location on the boat, and it is advisable to make out a deviation card showing the errors for different bearings.

The fathometer is often not used to full advantage in fog piloting. It is useful not just to warn of shoal water but also for running a chain of soundings to help establish your position. To use this method, steer a straight course at a fairly slow but steady speed and note soundings at regular intervals, perhaps every quarter of a mile. Draw a straight line representing the course on a sheet of tracing paper (or on the very edge of a piece of opaque paper), and mark along the line the quarter-mile distances (to the same scale as your chart) with the soundings. Then place the paper on the chart in your approximate location; orient the line to the course direction; and shift the paper around until the recorded soundings correspond with those on the chart.

Another way to make use of the depth sounder is to run a fathom line—that is, steer the boat to follow one of the fathom lines (lines joining soundings of equal depth) that appear on the chart. It takes a good deal of hunting (trial-and-error course changes) to keep the depth readings the same, but it is perfectly possible to stay close to a line that is not overly tortuous. Very often a fathom line will lead you close to a prominent buoy. Incidentally, if the buoy produces sound but you cannot hear it when you are under power, shut off the engine at frequent intervals to improve audibility.

Common Crises

Serious emergencies such as capsizings, dismastings, fire, collisions, man overboard, steering casualties, and the like were discussed in my book *Sea Sense*, but here I would like to pay some attention to a few of the more common, usually less serious kinds of accidents that so often plague the inexperienced or overly casual cruising sailor. Many of these minor crises (fouled or dragging anchors, gear spilling from shelves or lockers, fouled lines, chafe problems, sail handling difficulties, certain docking errors, and so forth) have already been discussed in this book, but what remain to be touched on are such problems as a fouled propeller, jammed halyard, winch overrides (from the standpoint of clearing), clogged head, balky stove, running aground, and dinghy misbehavior.

During the early part of my sailing career, I had several misadventures involving fouled propellers. In my particular case, the reason for the accident was always that the dinghy painter had become wrapped around the prop when the engine was in reverse. Later I put cork floats on the painter and had no further trouble. After each accident I was lucky enough to be able to clear the prop by pulling on the painter while the engine was run slowly in forward gear. Of course, the gear would have been shifted to reverse to clear if the prop had fouled while going ahead. It is probably a better idea, however, to shut off the engine promptly after the prop is fouled (sometimes it will shut itself off) and try to rotate the prop shaft by hand to unwind the line. In many cases the fouled line cannot be unwound and will have to be cut free. A snorkel mask and a heavy, sharp knife are useful for this, but it has been suggested that a very tightly wrapped line is best cut with a hacksaw. In some cases when the line is extremely jammed the internal coupling bolts on the shaft might have to be released to allow the shaft to be slid aft to loosen up the jam.

Needless to say, painters are not the only things that can foul a propeller. A loose sheet lying on deck and falling overboard, for instance, can easily get sucked into the prop. Generally speaking, one should always see that slack lines are pulled taut, coiled, and hung or securely stowed. Loose lines not only are vulnerable to getting caught in the prop, but they also can catch on any prominent object, become kinked or knotted, and cause a person to trip.

Halyards usually jam because the wire has jumped out of its sheave and become wedged between the sheave and the side of the block. Sheaves intended for wire halyards with rope tails should have a deep central groove that will accept the wire, and as suggested earlier, it is often a good idea to have a keeper that will hold the halyard where it belongs when the sheave is inside the mast. At least there should be a separator between side-by-side masthead sheaves to prevent one halyard from jumping across to its neighboring sheave. This happened to me once when a squall was making up, and as a result, neither the mainsail nor the jib could be lowered. Beware of using wire halyards on laminated plastic sheaves, because I have seen these split open and jam the wire.

Halyard jams can be difficult to rectify, because usually no amount of hauling on the sail will make it come down. I heard of one case where an inexperienced skipper with a jammed halyard simply abandoned his boat after it was moored and let the sail flap itself to pieces. Rectification of this dilemma is normally best accomplished by brailing up the sail. When the jib cannot be lowered, pull the clew forward to the stay, roll up the foot, and stop it to the stay as far up as you can reach. Then take a free masthead halyard such as the spinnaker or spare jib halyard (or perhaps the fall of the halyard by which the jib is hoisted, if it is external) and wind it around and around the sail until it is subdued and in effect brailed to the stay (see Figure 6-8, A). If the jib has hanks it will be easier to wrap the sail and keep the turns of halyard in place. Later, after the boat is moored or at least taken into smooth water, a man can be sent aloft in a bosun's chair to unsnap the halyard, and the sail can be unwrapped and lowered. The jam might be cleared from aloft, but the block or sheave may have to be removed if the wire has been very forcibly pulled down.

If the main halyard should happen to jam, perhaps the outboard end of the boom can be pulled aloft with the topping lift. Robin Knox-Johnston did this when his halyard jammed during his famous single-handed circumnavigation, but first he slacked off the tack area by unrolling his reefed main to

FIGURE 6–8: JAMMED HALYARD AND WINCH

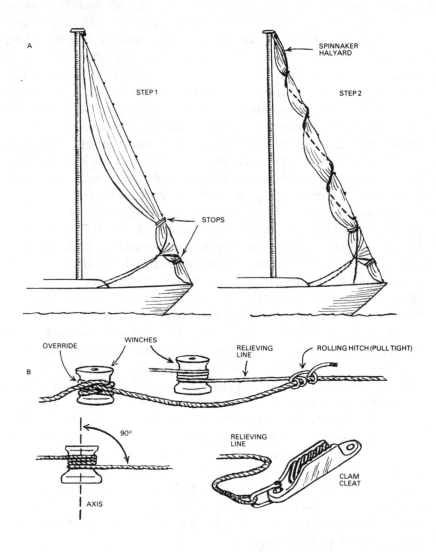

prevent the sail from tearing. Then he topped up the boom and "frapped the sail to mast and boom." If the boom cannot easily be lifted, of course, the foot will have to be removed from the boom so that the sail can be brailed against the mast.

Sheet jams are most often caused by kinks in the line or

overrides on winches. Kinks jamming in jib sheet lead blocks are best avoided by carefully coiling or flaking down the line. On a racing boat it is often best to assign a crew member the job of seeing that the windward sheet is clear immediately after coming about, while the leeward sheet is being winched in. As mentioned in Chapter 1, overrides most often result from improper leads to the winch, usually from leading the sheet down to the winch rather than leading slightly up or having the line make a right angle to the turning axis of the drum. Another cause of overrides is putting too many turns of the sheet around the winch when it is being hauled in hand-over-hand before cranking. It is usually best to put only two or three turns around a standard sheet winch while hauling in a sheet rapidly. One wrap lets the sheet slip too easily, and the sheet tender is in danger of having his hand pulled against the winch, where it could be pinched under the line.

Once the sheet has jammed, it is nearly always necessary to take the strain off the kink or override in order to clear it. If it is not blowing too hard, this can be done by merely gripping the sheet by hand forward of the jam and pulling aft to put slack in the line so that the jam can be cleared. When it is blowing hard, slack will have to be obtained with another winch. The usual method of doing this is to tie a relieving line to the sheet to take the strain. The relieving line is attached to the sheet with a rolling hitch, or it may be attached by using a clam cleat jammed on the sheet and held there by hand (Figure 6-8, B). The clam can be secured to the end of the relieving line with a small steel shackle as illustrated. If there is no secondary winch to relieve strain on the sheet, a tackle (perhaps the boom vang) can be used.

Many a cruise has been made considerably less delightful than it could have been by a broken or clogged head (toilet). The usual reason for this is failure of the skipper to give his crew or guests proper instructions for using this delicate mechanism. Complete, clearly written instructions should be posted in plain view near the toilet, and all guests should be told to read them and to ask questions if there is any possibility of a misunderstanding.

On several occasions I have heard of the toilet's outlet line being ruptured because someone pumped violently without first opening the seacock. Of course, these accidents could have been avoided with simple instructions. Probably the most usual problem with the head is clogging after someone has tried to pump foreign objects through the outlet line. The most common culprits seem to be women's sanitary devices. Nothing should be thrown in the bowl except a minimum of toilet paper, and your instructions should spell this out. Once the head is really clogged, about the only remedial action is to close off the seacocks, remove the outlet line, and ream it out with a piece of heavy wire. Be sure to carry adequate wrenches and spare parts for the head and other important mechanical equipment as well. You should carry a wrench large enough to fit the largest nut on the boat. And incidentally, keep all nuts tight.

Another piece of equipment that can put a damper on the full enjoyment of a cruise is a balky stove. The majority of small to medium-sized American cruisers are fitted with alcohol pressure stoves. These are fine when they are working properly, but quite often dirt or corrosion and improper adjustment can cause annoying problems. Obviously, the manufacturer's instructions should be read and followed very carefully, and the stove should be kept clean. There is usually an automatic provision for cleaning a clogged burner nozzle by turning the control knob for the burner all the way to the left (counterclockwise), sending a needle through the jet to improve the quality of the flame. This may have to be done fairly often, and you must be sure there is no buildup of dirt or corrosion that will prevent full penetration of the needle. Another cause of imperfect flame is a wrong air-to-fuel ratio. The mixture can usually be adjusted with a calibration disc under the burner caps. Exact instructions for regulation are normally included with every new stove.

Perhaps the most common problem with alcohol stoves comes from flare-ups of the flame. Flare-ups are nearly always due to insufficient priming or occasionally to reignition of unvaporized alcohol after the flame has blown out. Before lighting a burner, be sure it has been thoroughly preheated (with alcohol, pellets, or alcohol paste burned in the cup under the burner), and don't try to light the stove in a very strong draft. See that there are no curtains or towels hanging above the stove that could be ignited and always have a *large* pot of water handy before lighting (alcohol fires can be put out with water, but be sure to use plenty to prevent smoldering).

Running aground was covered in some detail in *Sea Sense*, but this type of accident seems to be such a common occurrence when gunkhole cruising that a few of the more common errors made in freeing the boat after grounding should be mentioned here. Probably the most common mistake when a boat grounds under sail is failure to drop sail at once. Occasionally the boat can be tacked immediately after touching the bottom, and then perhaps she can be heeled over and driven off under sail; but in the vast majority of cases she cannot be turned before solidly grounding, and then the sails will drive her further onto the shoal. Since it may take a few minutes to lower sail, slack the sheets right off at once so that the sails will lose their thrust. An exception to dousing sail early, however, might be in the case of a very serious coastal grounding in heavy seas where the lives of the crew are in jeopardy, and the boat can be driven close to shore by keeping her sails filled. Also, where there is a narrow sandy bar, the boat might be driven over it into deeper and perhaps more protected water, but these cases are rare in normal gunkhole cruising.

After grounding on a hard bottom it is important to inspect the bilges to see that the hull has not been holed. I have heard of several cases where a grounded boat has been freed, only to sink in deep water. If the boat has not been damaged, obviously you should make an attempt to move her toward the deep water, but be sure you know where it is. Quite often grounded boats are driven or pulled in the wrong direction. No freeing action should be taken until you study the charts carefully and/or take soundings (usually from a dinghy) all around the vessel. Sometimes people struggle to free their boats immediately after grounding when it would be much easier and perhaps cause less damage to take freeing action after the

A serious grounding. The usual rule for grounding is to lower sail at once so that the boat will not be driven further aground, but in a coastal grounding in surf where there may be a real risk of life, it might be better to leave the sails hoisted in order to drive the boat ashore so that the crew can easily evacuate. This particular vessel was abandoned at sea. (Photograph courtesy of *Salt Water Sportsman*.)

tide has risen. Of course, determining when such action should be taken will depend on the state of the tide at the time of grounding and on whether or not the boat is being damaged by seas.

Pivoting a grounded boat with a kedge anchor set out abeam off the bow is often an effective way of freeing her. The pivoting breaks the suction of the keel in a soft bottom and, of course, gets the boat turned toward deep water so that she can be driven ahead under power and sail. Often the sails can be sheeted in to maximize heeling (after the boat is headed the right way), and this will decrease the boat's draft. You should pivot a boat, however, *only* when the bottom is soft and when only a short length of keel is embedded in it, for I have heard of keels being twisted or otherwise damaged from pivoting action when their bottoms were wedged between rocks.

Heeling is sometimes induced by the careening method—that is, heaving down the boat with a line leading from the masthead to an anchor or tow boat some distance away and nearly abeam of the grounded vessel. Halyards are often used for this, but care must be taken to see that the masthead block is able to turn and swivel so that it can take the strain without jamming or breaking. The usual internal mainsail and genoa sheaves are not designed to take such side loads.

Other mistakes associated with grounding are overheating the engine by racing it too much or by not realizing that the cooling water intake has been lifted into the air; stirring up sediment from the bottom that is then sucked into the engine; attempting to free the boat with the rudder imbedded; using improper kedging technique; and attaching tow lines to weak fittings. The last point is especially important, because people have been seriously injured from fittings pulling off. Be sure that tow lines are secured only to heavy fittings that are through-bolted and have solid backing blocks of adequate area. In many cases a Sampson post or the base of the mast might be used, but then one has to be careful that chocks are well secured. When really severe strain is anticipated, the tow line should be secured to a bridle that passes entirely around the hull. By all means, never station yourself or a crew member where injury could be inflicted by the breaking of a fitting or the parting of the tow line.

As for kedging technique, the most common problems (aside from pulling the boat in the wrong direction) seem to be difficulties in setting out the kedge anchor, failure to trim or heel the boat properly before kedging, and failure to produce sufficient hauling power. The simplest way to take out the kedge in a dinghy is usually to carry the rode, especially one of chain, on the stern thwart of the dinghy rather than paying it out from the bow of the grounded vessel. The rode should be carefully coiled or flaked if the rode is braided line, and the anchor should be suspended outboard over the transom of the dinghy so that it can be quickly and easily dropped.

Once the anchor is set the boat should be heeled if possible and especially trimmed to lift the deepest part of the keel. Normally this would mean moving heavy weights and extra crew to the bow. Of course, the skipper ought to be thoroughly familiar with the underwater configuration of his boat. Incidentally, it is a good idea on long cruises to carry complete plans of the boat that show her keel profile, prop location, rudder shape, position of transducers or sensors, and so forth. When the grounded boat is being pulled off a soft bottom, she should be rocked as much as possible in order to break the suction of the imbedded keel.

Kedging power may be increased by leading the anchor rode to the most powerful winch. Of course, a fairly small-diameter rode should be used, and the lead blocks must be strong and well secured. Some modern sailors tend to overlook the efficacy of a proper tackle. In my opinion a handy billy (a small, general-purpose tackle) should be carried on every boat. Combining a tackle with a large sheet winch can produce considerable power. Obviously, the engine should also be used to augment the purchase and winch power when possible

If the boat should happen to ground where there is an extreme tide, care must be taken not to let her fall over on her side at low water. Boats have been damaged, because they were not properly lashed or shored upright. If it is not possible to keep the boat upright, let her heel as the tide goes out and put padding under her side where it will rest on the ground.

Another common source of trouble when cruising is the dinghy. Problems other than getting its painter caught in the propeller (which has already been discussed) are losing the dinghy when it is being towed, having it swamp or yaw wildly while under tow, and having it bump the topsides of the mother vessel at night when she is anchored. The simplest solution for all these problems is to carry the dinghy on board in proper chocks.

The larger cruising boats often have davits, usually at the stern, to simplify bringing the dink aboard, but the operation is really not too difficult without davits when the topsides of the mother vessel are not extremely high. The dink is brought alongside, and two persons standing at the rail can lift the small boat aboard by pulling up on the painter and a stern line made fast to the stern thwart or a transom ring. A great many cruising sailboats can carry the dinghy upside down on chocks fastened to the cabin top. Just be sure it is lashed in place securely. It is often a good idea to have the lashing lines or holding straps fastened to eyes or holes in the chocks with snap shackles so that the dinghy can be released immediately in case it is needed as a lifeboat.

When the cruiser is too small to carry a solid dinghy on board, an inflatable boat can usually be carried. Very often it is successfully carried partially inflated and folded over so that it will take up less room. Be sure the inflatable is always attached with its painter to the mother boat, because inflatables are very light and they are famous for blowing overboard in a strong wind. They can even blow upside down while afloat when no one is on board; so don't leave the oars and other gear aboard, and don't leave an outboard motor attached to the stern for very long.

When a dinghy must be towed, be sure there is a painter of ample length attached to a bow eye that is through-bolted, and see that the eye is sufficiently low that the bow can be lifted slightly to alleviate yawing. In following seas, which make yawing a real problem, a small drogue towed astern of the dinghy can be helpful. A small cloth sea anchor (like the kind used with horseshoe buoys but with a little weight added) might be used for the drogue. It can be placed on the bow thwart as illustrated in Figure 6-9, so it can be reached with a boathook after the dink has been pulled in close to the stern of the mother boat.

Perhaps the greatest difficulty one can have with a dinghy is to have it swamp while it is being towed. This usually happens because of a sudden change in weather or sea conditions or sometimes because of a daggerboard well that gradually admits water. Sailing dinks must have tight-fitting well caps held securely with large cotter pins or by some other means, and most dinghies should have a watertight gasket around the top of the well.

FIGURE 6–9: TAMING A WILD DINGHY

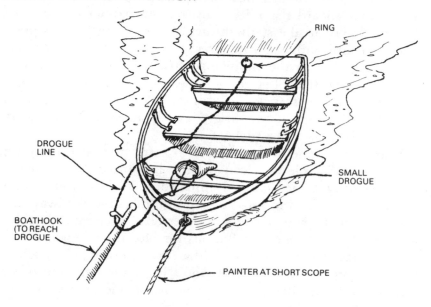

I was once caught in a bad storm that came up suddenly while the dinghy was being towed. Being short-handed, I could not bring the dinghy aboard, and it swamped. During the blow, which had gusts of over sixty knots, we ran off under bare pole, and the dinghy behaved as if it had gone berserk. First it would tumble and roll down the face of a sea, and then it would dive like a sounding whale. Fortunately, I had a strong nylon painter of considerable length securely attached to a heavy bow eye that was bolted through a large backing block; and we never lost the dink although the storm lasted for several hours. However, we did lose the oars and oarlocks. The lessons I learned from that experience were: (1) Always bring the dinghy on board unless you are certain there will be no bad weather or difficult seas. (2) Be sure there is a long painter in case you get caught towing the dink in bad weather, because at short scope the boat can be thrown by following seas against the stern of the mother vessel. In addition, a long nylon painter lessens shock loading. (3) Always remove oars, oarlocks, and other loose gear from the dink if you plan to tow it.

Before concluding, I would like to offer some advice about accidents that can cause injury. Injuries most often result from improper handling of lines and from falls. To avoid the former, a few general rules (of which some have already been mentioned) are as follows:

- Always keep lines carefully coiled or flaked.
- Keep cleated lines reasonably taut when excessive slackness can cause fouling.
- Never stand in a coil or position yourself directly behind or in the bight of a line under strain.
- Don't operate a winch, especially a reel type, without understanding how it works. If you are the skipper, be sure to caution and instruct all crew or guests.
- Always handle a line under strain (or one that will come under strain) with a turn around a cleat and at least two turns around a winch.
- Be extra careful about snubbing an anchor rode or a tow line. Be sure there is plenty of slack before taking a turn around the cleat or bit so that you cannot pinch a finger.
- Keep your back as straight as possible when lifting a heavy anchor. Use engine power rather than your back to break out the hook.
- Use lines of ample diameter for firm gripping to avoid rope burns.
- Never grab a runaway line or hold a line close to the swallow of a block or chock (the swallow is the aperture through which the line passes).

With regard to falls, observe the following rules:

- See that companionway ladders are well secured.
- If you remove a companionway ladder, warn everyone on board and close the sliding hatch.
- See that all hatches are closed when sails are furled and headsails are lowered.
- Do not leave loose sails lying on the deck. Furl and stop or bag them.
- Skidproof all slippery surfaces and see that the boat has ample grab rails above and below deck.

- Always look where you are walking.
- Warn your crew, especially those below, when your boat will encounter powerboat swells or a patch of rough seas.
- If you are at the helm, always give ample warning before you come about, jibe, or make a sudden turn when under power.
- See that lifelines are taut and, of course, that the whole assembly is strong. Don't sit on them or fend off a boat by her lifelines.
- Don't try to fend off a heavy boat moving against a dock with your foot, as this might result in a fall or a crushed foot. Use a fender.
- Bear in mind the ancient admonition, "one hand for the ship and one for yourself."

As I pointed out earlier, mistakes can never be eliminated entirely because of the vagaries of wind, water, and boat. On top of these are the normal failings of the human mind. However, we can learn from our own mistakes and those of others sufficiently well to keep our troubles to a minimum. Perhaps the main reason sailing is such a fascinating challenge is that, regardless of one's experience, there is always the potential for mistakes and there is always something new to be learned.

Index